The Broad Road

A Story of Two Paths of Eternal Consequence

Ben Newell with Marvin J. Newell

WESTBOW
P R E S S®
A DIVISION OF THOMAS NELSON
& ZONDERVAN

Scripture taken from the Holman Christian Standard Bible ® Copyright © 2003, 2002, 2000, 1999 by Holman Bible Publishers. All rights reserved.

Scripture taken from the Holy Bible, NEW INTERNATIONAL VERSION®. Copyright © 1973, 1978, 1984 by Biblica, Inc. All rights reserved worldwide. Used by permission. NEW INTERNATIONAL VERSION® and NIV® are registered trademarks of Biblica, Inc. Use of either trademark for the offering of goods or services requires the prior written consent of Biblica US, Inc.

Scripture taken from the New King James Version. Copyright © 1979, 1980, 1982 by Thomas Nelson, Inc. Used by permission. All rights reserved.

Scripture quotations are from The Holy Bible, English Standard Version® (ESV®), copyright © 2001 by Crossway, a publishing ministry of Good News Publishers. Used by permission. All rights reserved.

Scripture quotations taken from the Holy Bible, New Living Translation, Copyright © 1996, 2004. Used by permission of Tyndale House Publishers, Inc., Wheaton, Illinois 60189. All rights reserved.

WestBow Press books may be ordered through booksellers or by contacting:

WestBow Press
A Division of Thomas Nelson & Zondervan
1663 Liberty Drive
Bloomington, IN 47403
www.westbowpress.com
1 (866) 928-1240

Because of the dynamic nature of the Internet, any web addresses or links contained in this book may have changed since publication and may no longer be valid. The views expressed in this work are solely those of the author and do not necessarily reflect the views of the publisher, and the publisher hereby disclaims any responsibility for them.

Any people depicted in stock imagery provided by Thinkstock are models, and such images are being used for illustrative purposes only. Certain stock imagery © Thinkstock.

ISBN: 978-1-5127-1137-0 (sc)
ISBN: 978-1-5127-1138-7 (hc)
ISBN: 978-1-5127-1136-3 (e)

Library of Congress Control Number: 2015914572

Print information available on the last page.

WestBow Press rev. date: 09/16/2015

Contents

Introduction...vii

Chapter 1   Up, Up and Away 1

Chapter 2   "Not Have Time" and "Us"....................................14

Chapter 3   Working It Out...23

Chapter 4   The Other Side 36

Chapter 5   Crossing the Great Divide 50

Chapter 6   Confused and Refused.. 66

Chapter 7   The Narrow Road 74

Chapter 8   The Broad Road Ends...86

Chapter 9   Voices in the Dark 93

Chapter 10 Changing Your Final Destination.......................109

Notes 113

Introduction

For many, the thought of what happens after this life is over can be terrifying. Contemplating life beyond the grave can be scary. This is an unpleasant subject for most people. As such, they would prefer to avoid discussing it.

Truth be told, we spend most of our lives trying to avoid the unpleasant, the troubling, the scary. For instance, when the car engine begins to knock, we keep on driving, hoping the cause is bad fuel. Or if our chest develops a pain, or our stomach begins to ache, we first reach for a pill or antacid, hoping the discomfort is not serious. We would rather avoid dealing with anything that appears to be ominous until it is the last resort. Our initial reaction is to hope an issue or discomfort is not serious.

This book considers a subject that has troubled mankind from the beginning. It deals with the age-old question, "What happens to me after I die?" We spend our lives acting as if we are impervious to death even though there are daily reminders that we are not. Thinking about the end of life can be troubling, if not scary. We would rather avoid the subject altogether.

Yet, deep in our hearts we all have an opinion of what happens to people after they die. Some people believe that when you die, you are permanently terminated, both physically and spiritually, with no further existence. Some believe that most people go to heaven where they join the heavenly angels. Some individuals believe that there is a place called hell but that only bad people go there. And then there are those who believe that there is a heaven and hell, but there are different layers of pleasure and punishment that commensurate with one's behavior while here on earth.

Whatever your belief about the afterlife, there is one thing that is probably true of you – you haven't spent much time thinking about it. When you go to make a major purchase like a home or a car, every effort is taken to read the entire contract or purchase agreement. You might even hire a lawyer to help decipher the "small print" to make sure you are fully aware of what you are agreeing to. The most responsible thing to do is to know every detail and the bottom line cost.

Our intent in writing this book is to help you think more clearly about the end of your life. Instead of a belief in an afterlife based on popular culture or religious half-truths, we present to you the facts based on what God has told us, not what man has said, on this important subject.

Our fictitious traveler in this book will take you down the "Road of Life" that you will recognize. As he interviews people along the way, he will face long standing questions such as:

> Do heaven and hell really exist?
> What determines entry into each of those polar opposite places?
> Does a loving God send people to hell?
> How much do my good works matter?
> How is one assured that he is going to heaven?

These and other related topics are dealt with as our traveler progresses down the road and encounters people in all walks of life.

Since the day we are born, each one of us has traveled down this road. None of us know how long that road will be. Some are oblivious to where they are going, while others prudently check their bearings, constantly monitoring where they are headed. But we all know that our earthly existence will come to an end at some point in time. We just don't know when.

Our traveler interviews all sorts of people. Don't be surprised if you find yourself among them and he is talking directly to you. You most likely will face questions that you would rather avoid. We strongly suggest that for your own wellbeing and assurance, you work through those issues.

There is nothing more tragic than someone in crisis crying out in despair the words, "If I had only known." This is especially true when the information needed was readily available. This story is meant to provide you with vital information about your final destination before your life's journey comes to an end.

Ben Newell
Marvin J. Newell

CHAPTER 1

Up, Up and Away

It was the type of Saturday morning that made life worth living; the sun was shining and the air was pleasantly warm. As I pulled into the parking lot of the neighborhood Starbucks I could see that my coveted table on the sidewalk was empty. I parked up close to the door and hurriedly made my way into the shop. The weekend group was in its normal corner discussing the problems of the world. The rest of the patrons had their heads buried in their phones and thumbs were flying.

I usually ordered my standard bold house blend with no sugar or cream, but today was going to be different. To celebrate the beginning of fall, I had decided to go totally out of form and dive into one of those Pumpkin Spice Frappuccinos that were prominently displayed on large posters. As I ordered the drink and a chocolate scone, the girl behind the counter smiled and raised her eyebrows a bit, for she knew I was diverting from my normal fare and was taking a walk on the wild side. After paying and swiping my loyalty card, I quickly headed outside to the sidewalk to claim my round table. I settled into the cushioned chair with the sun to my back, pulled out my I pad, hit the New York Times icon and settled in for a relaxing hour. I took several sips of the drink and a bite of the scone and felt the effects of the sugar coursing through my body. As I leaned back, letting the sun and food work their magic, my body really felt weird, seeming to drift up and away from my chair. When I looked down at what had been the table, I now saw it morphing into something quite different. Oddly, it now represented the whole earth with me floating far above it! I was pulled so far up and away from it that I felt as if I was entering the stratosphere.

My first thought was that I had suffered a heart attack, had died, and my spirit was being sent straight to heaven. But something didn't quite add up. Wasn't that transition supposed to happen in a nanosecond? And wasn't I supposed to be whisked directly into the presence of the Lord? And why was I hovering above the earth like some sort of satellite? *No*, I thought, *I must not be dead after all.*

The scene below me didn't make sense either. What I took for being the earth did not look like it. It had no blue oceans covering two-thirds of its surface. It had no long winding rivers emptying into bluish green seas. I did not see the long Florida or Italian peninsulas or the great island of Australia. In fact, I couldn't distinguish any geographical features whatsoever. It was very odd.

Neither did it look like a sphere glistening against a darkened universe, with sparkling stars from distant galaxies in the background. From wherever I was hovering, it had the shape of the table that I had been sitting at, perfectly round and mostly flat. It made no geographical sense to me. For a few minutes I was bewildered until it gradually dawned on me that I was observing earth from a totally different perspective.

The Great Circle

As I looked at what was originally the table, I saw at the center a large glowing mass. The light radiating from it was very bright and yet it did not burn my eyes. When they focused in on the glow, I felt thousands of emotions, all of them more joyful than the last. I could not see any part of my body but it felt as if every one of my molecules were enveloped in goodness. It was so peaceful and tranquil. I knew I never wanted to leave this experience. As I gazed on that lighted center, its sheer purity was seductively drawing me in. But suddenly something rudely pushed my eyes away from it. Immediately I felt a great let down, like someone had just offered me the greatest possible gift only to snatch it away.

Next, I felt myself drifting toward the distant perimeter of the great circle. I began to notice an orangey tint to its outer edge. As my eyes focused on that outer rim a strong sense of apprehension flooded over me. Something was terribly wrong there. My ears could faintly hear sounds of distress. Cries of great agony were rising through the atmosphere toward me. The air was filled with evil. Whatever was going on, I knew I had to get away or I would be consumed by it. With immense relief I was able to pull away from the rim and back to a more general overview of the astonishing spectacle below.

Keeping clear from both the center and the edge, I could distinguish dark moving masses. Long wide columns of something, still opaque to me, seemed to be marching toward that foreboding outer edge. The scene reminded me of the long lines of Brazilian army ants in the Amazon jungle, all moving with some kind of purpose streaming to the nest of a queen. They just mindlessly marched along, uninterrupted.

I could also see a much thinner line heading in the opposite direction, toward the center radiance. Other smaller groups were just swirling around but gradually making their way to the edge. Everything that I was observing was so confusing! Was I daydreaming or was I actually actually observing something that was real?

I decided that since nothing below me made any sense, I needed to get closer to clearly observe what was actually going on. How to do that was the next question. I needed to find out if I could maneuver my body in this suspended state. Could I shoot straight in the air, sort of like Superman? Try as I might, nothing happened. Could I make precision turns like the Navy's aerobatic team, the Blue Angels? Again, I tried, but nothing happened. It dawned on me that maybe this experience was not for my entertainment. With a little experimentation, I found that I could move to the center and to the edge and downward. So those being my only options, I headed down to discover what the dark masses were that were crawling along.

On the Road

Almost instantly I was on the ground among fellow human beings. They all seemed to be in a hurry to get somewhere and most of them were headed in the same direction on a very broad road. I tried hailing someone's attention to find out where they were going, but nobody paid attention to me. I flailed my arms, jumped up and down, and screamed at the top of my lungs— all to no avail. No one paid attention to me whatsoever. I even tried to step directly in their way but they seemed to go right through me. This was very weird.

I really wasn't sure what kind of state I was in. Could this all be a wild dream? Could these people even see me? It became obvious that I was going to have to answer these questions if I were to understand this experience.

Now, if I could only communicate with someone on the road that would be a start. Since I was not making any headway in getting anyone's attention, I was left with no alternative but to move along with the crowd to discover where they were going. Hopefully it wouldn't be far.

As we moved along, it wasn't long until I could see a large well-lit sign overhead that spanned the wide avenue. It held a huge rectangular message board. As I approached it, I could readily read what was projected. In flashing red words it read:

"YOU ARE ON THE ROAD TO ETERNITY!"

As the multitude I was now a part of approached and passed under the sign, it was evident that they didn't even notice it. *How could they miss something so obvious?* I wondered.

As I looked closer, I could see that even though everyone was moving down the same road, they were engaged in all the various activities that humans have done since time began. They were playing, working, eating, or socializing. Interestingly, even when they were sleeping they were progressing down the road. Each was engaged in their own activities and yet all kept moving down the "Road to Eternity." Every stage of life was represented, from suckling babies to senior adults, with every age in between. There was no rest stop, and no one got off the thoroughfare to go somewhere else. They just kept moving straight ahead.

The road reminded me of a super-wide interstate with multiple lanes, similar to a road one would take when going to a major city. But there was a major difference—it was all one-way, going only in one direction. I strained to see if there were any reverse lanes going the opposite direction, but as far as I could see there were none. Everyone was headed in the same direction—nothing and no one was coming back toward me.

Looking down at my feet I noticed that the road was well maintained. I thought I saw a small sign along the side that said, "This mile has been adopted by the Local D Club." I also thought I saw a small yellow smiley face on it, but I wasn't sure. Too many people crowded the way. I wondered what the Local D club was.

The Divided Roads

Not far after passing the big sign, the road became divided into two sections. There was the crowded multi-lane highway on the left, and a much narrower single lane on the right. Both were clearly marked. The broad road had another flashing sign overhead that read,

"CAUTION, THIS ROAD LEADS TO HELL!"

The narrow lane had a sign that flashed,

"TAKE THE CROSSOVER: THIS ROAD LEADS TO HEAVEN!"

As everyone streamed pass the two signs, I was perplexed at how the masses just trudged right along, mostly ignoring both signs. The majority of the people were so busy with their typical affairs of life that they never took notice. Or if they did, it didn't seem to make any difference. I occasionally observed a few lonely souls break off at the crossover and join the heaven lane. It may have been my imagination but it looked like when they first broke away from the main road that there was an extra spring in their step and a radiance of joy on their faces.

I noticed that even though the lanes were separated, they ran parallel to each other. People could communicate and interact with each other across the lanes, and they did. There seemed to be an invisible barrier that no one could cross but I could not make out what it was. Some people in the hell lane stayed close to the heaven lane.

Others seemed to want to get as far away from it as they possibly could. They stuck to the outside express lane where they could get to their final destination faster without obstructions getting in their way.

The Broad Road

I decided I needed to follow the masses down the broad road to see if I could discover why they were intent on taking that route. As I did, I noticed a road construction crew ahead, spreading a new surface on one of the lanes. It made the surface very smooth and easier to travel on. Being involved in construction in my pre-hovering life, I wondered what they were putting in the mix to make the road so silky smooth. The crew that was operating the surfacing machine were wearing ball caps with a big red "D", They seemed friendly and would wave at the people passing while they worked. But the more I looked, the more sinister they seemed to me.

The crew was using a very large machine that was smoking from the hot mix inside its belly. On its side was written the warning, "Caution, Hot, Just the way we like it." One of the workers was adding a five-gallon can of liquid to the mix. I picked up an empty can that had been discarded and read "Good Intentions," written in big bold letters. On the back of the can was a list of ingredients written in small letters that included the following:

> "attend church more often"
> "increase the amount of money given to the less fortunate"
> "join a non-profit"
> "obey the law"
> "read the Bible or at least keep one in your house"
> "be tolerant"

The list went on and on.

It was difficult to observe, but on the side of the paving machine was a laser level that was constantly being checked by what must have been the crew chief of the "D" workers. It looked as if he was checking to make sure that the road had a slight decline to it. Every so often I saw another sign hanging across all the lanes that read:

TOLL ROAD: BE PREPARED TO PAY WHEN YOU EXIT

I now found that I could now communicate with the travelers. Maybe it was because I was moving along with them. I heard one who had actually noticed the sign, question a D worker as to the amount of the toll at the end of the road. He was concerned that he wouldn't have enough to pay the toll.

"Don't worry about that at all," replied the D worker with a grin, "you will have enough. And just to relieve your worries, I'm going to give you this Easy Pass. This will guarantee you won't have any problems paying at the end of your journey."

This seemed to satisfy the questioner, so he headed on down the road with the Easy Pass in hand. Out of the corner of my eye I caught the two D's laughing and slapping each other on the back, like they had just pulled off the greatest of jokes!

As I trudged along, I found that it was very difficult for people to have meaningful conversations with each other. While most of the time all I heard was a constant drone of voices, every once in a while I could pick out specific words. Words pertaining to the normal things of life such as money, teams, family, recreation, health, job, party, retirement, sex, and food were among those that were frequently audible above the din. Strangely, it seemed like they were just jabbering, rarely looking each other in the eyes as they talked.

Even though a few were engaged in conversation with each other, there didn't seem to be much listening. For the most part, they were only focused on themselves. I found the only way I could converse with anyone was to get right in front of them and almost shout in their ear. At least that way I could get them to acknowledge that I existed. It was at least a start.

Without trying to be too confrontational, I picked out a few people and asked them if they knew where they were headed. At first they would nod, but try to ignore me. Some tried to shove me out of the way, but I persisted in maneuvering myself in front of them, determined to get an answer.

In order to get me out of their face, many would respond with statements such as: "Well, friend, not that it's any of your business, but I'm just trying to move on through life, doing the best I can," or "Does it really make a difference? We're all going to end up in the same place anyway." These individuals had no idea where they were going and didn't seem to care.

I was surprised at my own tenacity to get answers. I could not recall that I had ever tried to pin a person down on the topic of eternity before my non-hovering experience. *Why should I care now?* I wondered. Yes, I had accepted Christ as my Savior as a youth and had always felt sure of my final destination, but I was rarely concerned about anyone else's. That was something they needed to worry about, not me.

I decided that if I was to understand this experience that I needed to be more confrontational. When we came to one of the many signs that said "YOU ARE ON THE ROAD TO HELL," I grabbed the face of a person next to me and made them look directly at the sign. I then had them read it aloud to me. For some reason I was not worried about the distinct possibility of being punched, or worse, being a nuisance. When I asked what they thought the sign meant, they simply shrugged their shoulders and said that they did not have a clue. Then off they went, continuing on their journey. I tried this with several people and got the exact same response.

Reflection: Is Hell Real?

When pollsters ask the question, "Is hell real," the American public overwhelming acknowledges a belief in hell (69% according to the May 2007 Gallup poll). However, they do not believe that they themselves could possibly be going there (25%).[1] But we are starting at the wrong place, because polls have very little to do with objective truth; instead, polls generally indicate how people feel at the moment.

On September 10, 2001, very few Americans believed that terrorists would destroy the Twin Towers in New York City. On September 11, Americans faced the reality that it was not only possible it was actual! If we want to uncover truth, we must rely on an unchanging source instead of people's subjective feelings, and there is no better source than the words of the Son of God, Jesus, recorded in His Holy Word, the Bible.

Jesus and Hell

Jesus spoke more about hell and its danger than anyone else in the Bible. He knew how terrible a place hell was and He made it clear to those who listened to Him, and now those who read His words, that it should be avoided at all cost. In Mark 9:43, He describes it as a place of "unquenchable fire." In Matthew 8:12 he describes it as a place of complete darkness, where there will be "weeping and gnashing of teeth."

Recently at a birthday party for a well-known, scruffy-looking country singer, a member of an old rock band proposed a toast to the honoree. In it he said, "I hope we have twice as much fun in hell as we have had in this life." This toast led to resounding cheers from the attendees and a cheerful uplifting of glasses.[2]

Think about Jesus' description of hell once again: sitting in utter darkness . . . not seeing anyone around you . . . tormented by flames . . . listening to yourself and others crying out in pain. This does not sound like something you should toast about! We should all pray that those two band members, and others like them, never experience the everlasting torment of hell.

Jesus gave a parable, recorded in Luke 16:19–31, about a rich man who dies and immediately experiences the anguish of hell. The rich man cries out for relief and after hearing that none will be coming, he pleads for a beggar, Lazarus, who has also passed and is now on the heaven-side of eternity, to go back to his living brothers and implore them to change their ways so they won't end up where he is. His experience is so painful that he does not wish it on anyone else, especially those dearest to him.

Consider this sobering question: Is it possible that you have a friend or relative experiencing the torments of hell at this very moment? Could they be sorrowfully hoping and pleading that you will not experience the same? Could there be someone screaming your name, hoping that somehow you will hear them and change your life's course?

Jesus even condemns some of the religious leaders of His day "to the judgment of hell." He rightly accused them of falsely distorting the truth of God and His message to His people (Matthew 23:33). What would He say today to many church leaders who teach that there is no literal place called hell, but that Jesus was just using that term metaphorically to implore listeners to be better people? In other words, some church leaders say that Jesus resorted to scaring those listening to Him in order to get them to change their ways and live with Him in eternity.

A few references have already been stated where Jesus mentions the dire eternal consequences of not believing in Him. He makes at least twenty such statements. What's more, hell is referenced throughout the Bible from beginning to end. Its dreadful reality is brought to concluding description in Revelation chapter 21, where the final judgment is described. There it says that people whose names are not found written in the "Book of Life" are cast into the eternal lake of fire along with Satan, their leader. This is the greatest tragedy of all tragedies.

Hell's Purpose

It must be remembered that God created hell for Satan and his fellow rebels who had connived to take over their Creator's exalted position. Satan is fully cognizant of the fate that awaits him when God brings an end to this present age. Thus, he takes great pleasure in blinding the eyes of as many humans as he can as to whom God is. Satan is occupied with scheming to take with him as many of God's best creation as he possibly can to join his eternal fate.

In C.S. Lewis' *Screwtape Letters*, the head demon is giving out instructions on how to deceive the people of whom the lesser demons are in charge. First he tells them to get the people so busy that they don't think about spiritual things. If that doesn't work, get their charges to question what is being taught. Also, get them thinking about what other people would think about them if they became a believer in God. And if worse comes to worse, where some do become believers, start back at the beginning and get them busy with other things so that their faith begins to wear off.[3] An assessment of the previously mentioned poll seems to indicate that Satan and his minions are doing a pretty fine job!

Jesus' Concern

Even though Jesus talked plainly and often about the reality of hell, we cannot ignore the fact that He spent most of His earthly ministry showing how much He loved people with a determination to keep them from it. He healed them, fed them, and even entertained with them. He taught truths to them, associated with the outcasts, and wept with His closest friends. He befriended everyone, ministering without discrimination.

Finally, in His last breath while in agonizing pain, He gave hope to a repentant crucified criminal, reassuring him that together they would soon be in paradise. He then died, taking the punishment of mankind for all our sins upon Himself so that someday we too would enjoy eternity in heaven with Him. Why God loves us so much that He desires to save us from an eternity in hell is a great mystery. But the fact of the matter is that He does love us, and He demonstrated that love by offering Himself in our place, on the cross.

Although we humans hate the thought of hell, we have no choice but to believe that it really exists. Why? Because Jesus taught it as a literal reality. As John Wesley convincingly said, "We give Scripture primacy, and Jesus spoke about hell."[4] Now, if we choose not to believe what the Bible says that Jesus taught about hell, then we have no reason to believe anything it says about heaven either, or anything else for that matter.

Study Questions

1. Do you believe we are all on an eternal journey or are you of the persuasion that someone's trip (existence) ends with the finality of physical death?

2. Have you thought much about hell and its implications for you personally? Why or why not?

3. What disturbs you the most about dying? Are you afraid of dying?

4. What makes the "Road to Hell" smooth for you personally?

5. Have you ever told anyone that you are assured that you are going to heaven and then ask if they are too?

6. Is it any concern to you if someone is headed down the wrong road?

   What does Jesus say? Read Luke 16:19–31.

CHAPTER 2

"Not Have Time" and "Us"

N.H. Time

I finally got one older person to talk to me. He told me his name was
N.H. Time. When I asked N.H. if he believed that he was on the road to
hell, he gave me a little smile and replied, "No, I don't think so. I don't
believe in a place called hell. A loving God would never send anyone
to a place like that, especially for an eternity."

When I asked him what he based his information on, he replied,
"I was baptized as an infant, went to church as a child, and attended
Christmas and Easter services as an adult. At those services all they
talked about was how 'God is love.' Therefore, unless the church
was lying to me, it would be illogical that a God of love would send
anyone to a terrible place like hell." Feeling pretty good with his
response, he put his head down and continued hiking down the
broad, straight road.

Not to be deterred, I caught up with him and again asked, "Do you
think that, in general, mankind believes in justice, Mr. Time?"

"Of course," he replied. "During my long life I've seen people do
some awfully bad things, and they deserved to be punished for them."

Trying to keep it simple, I continued, "Well, sir, justice is an
attribute of God, and He has instilled it into man. Yes, it is true that
God loves everyone, but He is terribly offended when humans reject
His great gift, the sacrifice of His perfect Son on the cross. Jesus died
for our wrongdoings. In fact, the Bible says that God is full of wrath
against those who reject His gift. Hell is justice for that rejection. The

bottom line is that man makes the choice. He can accept the gift of Christ's payment for sin and have eternal life in heaven, or receive his just due in a terrible place called hell."

The old-timer appeared to be contemplating the conversation, and then said, "You know, I've never heard it put that way before. While it kind of makes sense, I don't have time to deal with it now. I have been a very busy person all my life, and I still have a lot to do.

"I'm not getting any younger, you know," he concluded with a genuine smile on his face. And with that he shuffled on, disappearing into the busy crowd of people.

As I watched him go, I couldn't help but think that his road was probably going to end before he got around to changing lanes. *Where does Time go?* I wondered.

The Us Family

Next, a young family came along —father, mother, and three youngsters all under the age of six in tow. The parents looked intelligent and handsome, and all were well dressed. The children seemed to be happy, well cared for, and very active. They skipped, hopped, and twirled playfully as they merrily went down the road. Both parents seemed very attentive to the wishes and welfare of their brood.

I got up the nerve to break into their "quality time" by introducing myself. The father said that they were the Us family and that his name was All About, but his friends called him A.A. Pretending to be a pollster, I asked the parents what they were doing to care for their children's present and future safety.

My question was right up their alley! They proudly began to catalog all sorts of things they engaged in, such as checking the kids' toys to make sure they were safe; always buckling up in the car; feeding them food that was always nutritious. The few sweets that they gave to the children were tightly controlled—they were quite stringent about what the children were allowed to ingest.

They further informed me that each child already had a growing college fund. They even had a family secret password to use in case a pervert tried to steal one of them away. They showed me that, for further protection, they owned a backpack that had a string alarm that set off a screaming siren in case someone tried to snatch a child when he or she wasn't under one of their wings, which I thought was highly improbable.

"And yes," said A.A. as he looked at me suspiciously, "both my wife and I have plenty of insurance, if that is what you are selling."

Trying to gain their confidence, I assured them that I wasn't trying to sell them anything. I assured them I only wanted to ask a few questions. They agreed, so I started by asking them, "Do you know what road you are on, and where it leads?"

A.A. looked me squarely in the eyes and replied, "Of course we do. Do we look stupid?" Then, just to ease his own mind, he pulled out his phone, hit the GPS app, and smiled with satisfaction, signifying that they were just where he thought they should be.

Not to be deterred, I continued with my questioning. "What if I told you that you were on a very dangerous road, and you and your lovely family were all headed for impending disaster?"

Straightaway his wife gathered her offspring around her and, looking apprehensive, quickly glanced around to search out the hidden menace. A.A. quickly moved in front of them in a protective stance and asked, "What do you mean, sir? I don't see anything ahead that would remotely endanger my family—except possibly you!"

I took a step backward so as to be nonthreatening and pointed to the large sign ahead and responded, "According to that sign, you and your family are on the road to hell. That sounds pretty dangerous to me."

A.A. gave a chuckle and said with relief, "Oh, now I get it. You are one of those religious fanatics. You and your friends probably hung that sign yourselves. Well, let me tell you something. Amy and I are well-educated atheists, so we don't believe in God and we certainly don't believe in a place called hell. I can quote many highly educated and intelligent experts, both past and present, who hold the same belief. And I would appreciate it if you wouldn't mention that topic around our children. We don't want you scaring or confusing them with your archaic mystical beliefs."

I asked A.A. if he had ever been wrong about anything before. I detected a faint snicker from his wife, Amy, and then a brief glare from A.A. in her direction. Amy then jumped into the conversation with earnest.

"We used to be mostly meat eaters; in fact, we made great efforts to kill our own game with special hunting and fishing trips. But through research on the Internet, we have come to believe that being strict vegans is the best way to a healthy life. In fact, we legally named our littlest girl Radish," Amy said, beaming.

Hearing her name, the little one looked up at her mom with a smile. I had to admit she did seem to have a reddish glow to her skin. And she was a healthy-looking child.

"All right," A.A. broke in. "Getting back to the subject at hand, everyone has been wrong about something, including me, but I'm convinced that I am not wrong about this. Besides, you have no stronger evidence to back up your belief in God than I do for not believing in one."

"Oh?" I replied. "I can give you thousands of reasons to believe in God. I doubt if you can give me one good one not to, but back to my point: you have admitted to being wrong before. What if you're wrong about this most pressing question? What if there really is a just God, and the penalty for rejecting His great gift of love is an eternity in hell, separated from Him forever? If you're wrong, you've not only condemned yourself but you probably have condemned your precious little children to that same awful fate."

"That's an appalling thing to say!" Amy blurted. "How could you say something so mean, especially when you claim to be a Christian? We would never do anything to harm our children. And we intend to teach them when they are older to make up their own minds on such esoteric issues."

"I'm sure you will," I answered, "but just as they mimic you now, they will probably follow in your footsteps and in your beliefs as well. I've already warned you where this road is leading." Then, looking A.A. straight in the eye I pleaded, "Won't you please reconsider where you're leading them?"

"We've heard enough of this rubbish," A.A. gruffly replied. With that he wheeled around and herded his family together and then urged them on down the broad road.

As they moved away, I caught Amy, who was still holding on tightly to her children, glancing back at me. The anger was gone from her face, replaced with a look of concern.

Reflection: Is It Unloving to Tell Someone They Are in Danger of Hell?

One of the major obstacles in telling someone that if they don't put their trust in Jesus as their Savior they will go to hell for eternity is that we don't want to be perceived as unloving or offensive. All of us desire to be loved and accepted by those around us. If, in a moment of extreme anger, we tell someone to "go to hell," that's considered one of the greatest insults we can give.

If we truly believed that Jesus was telling the truth about this awful place of eternal torment, then we would never wish anyone to go there. So it stands to reason that if we believe in what Jesus repeatedly spoke about, we should do everything we can to make sure that our loved ones, acquaintances, and even total strangers are warned about this dreadful destination. If we saw one of our children about to put his hand on a hot stove, would we just shake our head and turn away unconcerned? Of course not!

English theologian John Blanchard relays this story in his book *Whatever Happened to Hell?* On December 12, 1984, dense fog shrouded the M 25 near Godstone, in Surrey, a few miles south of London. The hazard warning lights were on, but were ignored by most drivers. At 6:15 a.m. a truck carrying huge rolls of paper was involved in an accident. Dozens of cars were wrecked. Ten people were killed. A police patrol car was soon on the scene, and two policemen ran back up the motorway through the heavy mist to stop oncoming traffic. They waved their arms and shouted as loudly as they could, but most drivers took no notice and raced on toward the disaster that awaited them. The policemen then picked up traffic cones and flung them at the cars' windshields in a desperate attempt to warn drivers of the danger. One told how tears streamed down his face as car after car went by and he waited for the sickening sound of impact as they hit the growing mass of wreckage farther down the road.[5]

The Motive of Love

The plight of lost souls is so terrible, the power of sin so great, and the horror of hell so fearful, how can we possibly do nothing to warn people of their dangerous predicament and point them to the Savior? Far from being unloving when telling someone about hell, we are expressing love in its fullest sense. Love does not concern itself with temporary embarrassment. Neither is love telling someone what they want to hear. Real love is being concerned about someone's well-being and doing something about it. True love wants others to have what you have: the treasure of eternal life. Genuine love is doing the hard thing for the ones we care about, even if a "witnessing encounter" causes us a few moments of uneasiness.

Would you consider it unloving if, after an examination, your doctor informed you that unless interventional measures were taken, you were certain to die rather soon. Your reaction would be one of gratitude to him for not only finding what ails you, but also recommending a remedy. You would no doubt follow with serious discussion as to what must be done so that you might be cured.

The Great Physician has clearly stated that unless we accept His cure, we are doomed for all eternity. We have a choice when we hear this news. We can either become upset at the diagnosis, call Jesus a fraud, and go on living like we know better ourselves, or we can believe what He says and gratefully accept the cure that He has provided on our behalf.

Possibly you have seen the Seinfeld episode where Elaine finds out that her boyfriend regularly listens to Christian radio; he then informs her, in an offhanded way, that she is going to hell and he isn't. She is quite upset about the manner in which he gives her this information and that he is so nonchalant about it. Later, she forcibly exclaims, "If I am going to hell, you should care about it." Our friends have a right to feel the same way; "If hell is real, why haven't you told me about it? I thought we were friends."

How do we tell someone in a loving way that they are in danger of hell? Is standing on a soapbox and yelling the "bad news" effective? Would buying an ad on a major television network depicting flames of fire with people being tormented help viewers positively respond to the reality of their lost condition? Certainly not.

Example of Jesus

The best course of action is to follow Christ's example. We need to get involved in people's lives. We need to earn the right to speak. Befriending people, showing interest in their earthly concerns, and loving them unconditionally will cause them to be more open as you speak of their spiritual condition.

Charles Spurgeon said of our responsibility, "If sinners will be damned, at least let them leap to hell over our bodies: and if they will perish, let them perish with our arms about their knees, imploring them to stay . . . If hell must be filled, at least let it be filled in the teeth of our exertions, and let not one go there unwarned or unprayed for."[6] More of us need to apply Spurgeon's exhortation. We need to ask:

> In whose way are we intentionally standing while trying to get their attention to warn of their impending doom?
>
> Whose legs are we grabbing to prevent them from traveling on to impending disaster?
>
> In what way do we stand in oncoming traffic and try to warn travelers of the catastrophe that lies ahead of them?
>
> For whom are we wearing out our knees, beseeching God for the deliverance of their eternal souls?
>
> Do we shed tears as we see family and friends headed down a road that we know will end in eternal torment?
>
> Do we really love others, or do we just turn our backs and say, "Sorry, that's your problem"?

Study Questions

1. How can a loving God create a place as ominous as hell?

2. Why is it hard to get people to think about both heaven or hell?

3. What is justice? How does it play into the idea of eternal retribution?

4. How does our rejection of belief in God affect others who know us?

5. How would you react to being called a religious fanatic because of your witness?

What does Jesus say? Read Matthew 10:28, 32.

CHAPTER 3

Working It Out

Miss Taken

Standing there on the road to destruction, I figured I needed a better approach to get answers to my questions. So I picked up a short stick with a large, round knob on one end. Wielding it like a microphone, I shoved it into the face of a young woman who seemed to be having a jolly time as she headed down the wide road with a large group of similar, prim-looking young ladies. I got her attention by loudly announcing that I was a reporter for the local TV station, WLOST, and that I was doing a segment for an upcoming broadcast.

"We are trying to get viewers' opinions of hell, of all things. Would you mind answering a few questions for tonight's broadcast?" I asked.

While the young lady seemed puzzled that a TV station would be doing a story on this particular and rather morbid topic, she seemed quite pleased to know that she was going to be on the news. She started fixing her hair and straightening her clothes. Then her forehead furrowed as she silently pondered this tough subject. Because I've always secretly wanted to be part of the broadcast industry, I enthusiastically began my bogus interview.

"This is Chris Hoover reporting for WLOST News," I began as I pretended to look into a distant camera. "I have here a young lady who has agreed to talk to us tonight about our topic of the day, hell. . . . And what is your name, ma'am?" I asked, shoving the makeshift microphone into her face and hoping she wouldn't notice the deception.

"Cher Taken," she replied in a bubbly voice, trying to find the elusive camera.

"Well, Miss Taken, thank you for being willing to discuss this weighty topic. So what is your view of hell?"

She took a quick, deep breath. Glancing at her friends who were gathered to one side and smirking at her, she brushed back her hair and began her dissertation.

"I believe that hell is a totally terrible place, you know, and that only the worst people on earth go there. Mass killers like Hitler, you know, Osama Bin Laden and the sort. And certainly whacko mass murderers like that Adam creep who killed all those little children in Newtown, Connecticut and horrified our nation."

"Do you believe that you and your friends could be heading there right now?" I asked.

The young woman looked at me, aghast, like no one had ever asked her that before.

"Of course not!" she replied tersely. With fire in her eyes she continued, "I've never, you know, intentionally hurt anyone in my life! Like, I'm a good person. I always do good things. I wouldn't harm a flea. How could you even ask me that? Whatever!"

With that she abruptly ended the interview by turning and briskly walking on down the road with her giggling friends.

As I stood there dejectedly, with the imitation mic in my hand, it was evident that this new approach hadn't yielded its intended outcome.

Reverend Do

As I was trying to figure out what my next plan of action was to be, a group of decent-looking people began to pass by. They were obviously traveling together, and they seemed to be a quite jovial collection of people. I thought I heard a few of them singing some old-time church hymns. I asked a man who looked like he might be a leader what kind of gathering this was.

"Why, this is the First Church of Misconception," he retorted proudly. "We were the first church established in our community, well over a hundred and fifty years ago, and we have a large brick building located right on the main street of town. Our church has produced many outstanding leaders in our community, including four mayors. In fact, the current mayor is a deacon!"

The others in the group were nodding their heads, and it was apparent that this tightly knit group was very proud of its religious heritage and current prestigious status in the community. I was quite shocked to find this upstanding collection of people on this particular road. Outwardly, they seemed to be in the wrong place.

I couldn't help blurting, "How can this be? Don't you know what road you're on? This is the *road to hell*."

The spokesman looked at me, astonished at my pronouncement. "Oh, sorry sir, you are seriously mistaken." I glanced sideways, thinking the young lady was back.

"Look around you, sir," he continued. "You are looking at some of the finest people on the face of the earth. Most of them were born into the church. Over there is Matt, who is the president of our town's Lions Club and a long-term deacon in our church, as was his dad before him. You see that young lady over there? That is Mrs. Goodheart, and she is a Sunday school teacher, a mother of three, and head of the animal shelter. Oh, by the way, my name is Bourne Wright," he added, sticking out his hand and proceeding to give me a hearty shake.

"I myself was born into this wonderful church. My parents brought me every Sunday, even before I was born. I was baptized as an infant and received numerous attendance awards for my years in Sunday school. My wife and I were married in our beautiful building, and our kids went through all the programs that I did. I am now serving my fifth year as chairmen of the deacons.

"No one," he continued, "could be more plugged into religion than I am. There's no doubt in my mind that heaven is my ultimate destination.

"See that tall, distinguished man in the middle of the group with the broad smile on his face? That is our pastor. His full name is Reverend Do U. Feelgood. Everyone just calls him 'Rev. Do.' There couldn't be a more saintly man on the face of the earth. Every Sunday he preaches about how God is love and God wants us to love and help our fellow man. He preaches that we need to accept everyone no matter who they are, what they have done, what they believe, or what their orientation. Rev. Do started the community food pantry and regularly serves there himself. As his name suggests, he expects us to do things to help our fellow humans, too."

Mr. Wright gave me a wink and a nudge with his elbow. "And on Sundays, he preaches the message in twenty minutes." Then he said with a hearty laugh, "Got to beat the Methodists to the eateries!"

Looking over at Reverend Do, I could easily see that he was held in high esteem by those gathered around him. He was half a head taller than the others, and his broad smile seemed genuine. Even without knowing anything about him, I could see why people were drawn to him.

Making a sweeping motion with his arm toward his fellow congregants, Mr. Wright emphatically declared, "No sir, if these people aren't going to heaven, then no one is." With that, he put his arm on the shoulder of a young boy who obviously looked up to him and then blended into the joyful crowd that was moving down the thoroughfare. As they moved away, I could hear them singing a verse from *All You Need Is Love*.

After that conversation, I traveled behind the group by myself for a while. I began to have some doubts about where I was. These weren't the kind of people I would have pictured traveling on this road leading to destruction. None of them fit my perception of people who were heading to hell. All seemed to possess wholesome qualities; they weren't the rogues that normally come to mind as deserving the advertised destination.

As I followed them and pondered all this, I glanced over the invisible barrier to the narrow lane that the signage said was leading to heaven. I could see several people of this congregation moving along on that lane, but they were definitely in the minority. Even though everyone proceeded as one large group, I could definitely see the dividing line between the two groups. The smaller group on the heaven road didn't seem to be very concerned that their friends were on the wrong, broad road. Maybe they didn't know. Maybe they didn't care.

Professor K

Not far behind the Rev. and his flock was a group of young people who were well dressed and looked as if they hadn't a care in the world. They all had their eyes focused on a man in a sweater with glasses on a black string around his neck. You could tell they held him in high esteem, and it was also obvious that he enjoyed their admiration. He was expounding on some subject that I couldn't distinguish but the youthful listeners seemed to be hanging onto every word. I casually asked a young man on the fringe of the group who the distinguished-looking man was who held everyone so captivated.

"That's Professor K.I. All," he replied. "He's one of the most popular professors on campus. He always seems to know it all. He prefers that we call him Professor K."

Unnoticed, I fell in with the crowd so I could listen to what the professor was saying. One young lady in the enthralled group asked him, "Professor K, as chairman of the Department of Religion of our elite university, I would like you to expound on which is the true religion?"

He smiled and looked down at her. "Well, Darcy, that is a great and age-old question. As you know, I have dedicated my entire life to the study of religious beliefs, having two doctorates in the field. Most belief systems have a lot going for them, and I encourage my students to study them all to see which best fits them personally.

"While I wouldn't say that a particular one has all the truth, most of them have similar central themes that, if adhered to, would make the earth a much better place. I think we can all agree that if we treated fellow humans with kindness, and if we didn't kill or steal, and if we showed compassion to the poor, societies would be changed for the better. Most faiths deal favorably with these subjects."

Darcy must have been a freshman, for she wasn't afraid to continue with more pointed questions.

"I was brought up in a Christian home," she began, "and I was taught that Christianity is the only true religion and that the only way to heaven was to believe in Jesus Christ." A few scattered snickers could be heard from her classmates.

The professor looked amused. After taking a deep breath and making sure that everyone was turned toward him, he replied, "Now Darcy, I'm not here to change your religious beliefs in any way. I just want you to think about some implications." He paused for a few seconds to add to the drama. I could tell he was very good at what he did.

"What about all those hundreds of millions of people of different faiths?" the professor asked. "Are they automatically excluded from the reward of heaven just because they are not Christian? And all the good deeds they have done—do they mean nothing? And how about the billion or so people who have never heard of Jesus—are they excluded from heaven just because they were unfortunate enough to be born somewhere Christianity hasn't reached? I feel we are on dangerous ground when we become exclusive." Many in the group nodded their heads in agreement.

Undeterred, Darcy came back with, "Does that mean that Jesus was lying when He said, 'I am the way, the truth and the life. No man comes to the Father but by Me'?"

Professor K quickly retorted with annoyance in his voice, "I'm certainly not going to call Jesus a liar; but there is the possibility that the writers of the Bible may have overstated their case to make it more compelling."

Darcy was mulling that over when some signal occurred that I must have missed, because the group quickly began to disappear. The professor seemed glad to see Darcy go.

Only he and I remained, and I thought this might be my chance to have a good, scholarly discussion. As he was putting his papers in his briefcase, I moved next to him and said, "Professor, I couldn't help overhearing your discussion, and I was wondering if I could ask you a question."

"I suppose so, my good man," he replied without looking up. "I don't have another class until this afternoon." Then he made eye contact and said, "Fire away."

"I was wondering if you could tell me what road you are on," I asked. I could see that he was disappointed that I hadn't asked something more thought provoking. But he wasn't going to lose a chance to be philosophical, so he replied, "I guess that I am traveling down the 'road of life' like everyone else." He seemed quite proud of his answer.

"But do you know where this particular road ends?" I quizzed.

"I'm not sure what you are asking," he said with a puzzled look on his face.

I pointed to the sign that covered the massive road. "Can you read that sign up there?" I asked.

He looked up, squinted, and replied, "Certainly not without my glasses." And with that he placed his glasses that were suspended around his neck, and place them onto his nose. I could tell he was having trouble reading the large, red, flashing letters, and as I looked closer I saw the reason why. Written on both lenses were the words "great intellect." The thickness of the writing made it almost impossible for him to see through the lenses clearly.

I decided to help him out. "The sign says, 'You Are on the Road to Hell!'"

The professor's head snapped back and he looked at me in shock. Regaining his composure, he blurted, "First of all, I don't believe in hell. And secondly, even if there were such a place, I of all people certainly wouldn't be headed there. Don't you understand that one of my doctorates is in Comparative Religions? Also, I am a very good and well-respected person. Just ask anyone on campus. Also, I'm the head of the community United Way and regularly volunteer at the Salvation Army." With that he strolled down the road, muttering something about people who show no respect.

I couldn't help thinking that if I were him I would not be so determined to go further down this road.

Reflection: Who Is Going to Heaven, Who Is Going to Hell?

From the earliest of civilizations up until now, no matter the geographic location, humans have held as a common belief the twin destinies of hell and heaven. Without exception, every religion has a belief in the afterlife and eternal destiny. I (Marvin) discovered that every tribal group I encountered during my years ministering in Papua, Indonesia, believed in the afterlife.

Even today, polls show that most people believe that there are two distinct, final eternal destinations. Most believe that all humans are automatically bound for the better place. Most also believe that a person would have to do something heinous to be condemned to hell.

But most don't believe they could possibly be going there themselves. People have a short list of malevolent individuals they believe are going to hell, which usually includes past villains and the latest mass murderers found in the headlines. The evil actions of these extreme maniacs often make the common person feel better about their chances in light of eternity.

But instinctively we humans know that we're not good enough to deserve automatic acceptance into paradise at the time of death. So we try doing things that will qualify us for an entry pass. When these acts fail to make us feel secure and assured, we fall back on our own reasoning such as, "I'm not such a bad person, so a loving God couldn't possibly relegate me to a terrible place like hell."

The Trouble with Self-righteousness

Some religions teach that if, at the end of your life, the stack of "good deeds" is just a bit higher than the stack of "bad deeds," you have the right to enter heaven. Many non-Christians hold this theology (whether it's formalized or not). Their goal is to be labeled a "good person" by the end of life's journey. Their final destiny is assured, so they believe, based on their self-righteousness before God.

However, many questions are raised with this point of view. The trouble is that during one's lifetime one never knows how high each stack really is. For instance, what if something a person thought was good turned out to be bad in the eyes of the "Final Tally-er"? What if just one of someone's wrongs was so evil that it wiped out twenty good deeds? All calculations become rather subjective. And if they are subjective, then there is much room for error. And if there is room for error, there is little assurance one has calculated correctly regarding this, the most important equation in life.

In some early civilizations, some people went to the unbelievable extreme of sacrificing their own children to please the gods. They reasoned that giving up their most prized possession would earn them divine favor. Today we consider such notions horrendous acts of evil. But, who is right? What if you worked as hard as you possibly could to save yourself, only to discover that on Judgment Day you were one good deed short?

It's not difficult to see that any system based on works, merit, and self-righteousness is quite arbitrary and full of uncertainty. One reason people think a system of good works is the way to gain divine favor is that they can custom-design a merit system to fit their own particular biases and abilities. Too many are banking on the hope that their way, coupled with their efforts, will—in the end—gain them heaven. But even then, they don't know for certain.

That is why God has worked on man's behalf, providing a way of salvation in our helplessness. He shows mercy to us based not on our feeble efforts but on His grace. The Scripture puts it this way:

> But when the kindness and love of God our Savior appeared, he saved us, not because of righteous things we had done, but because of his mercy. (Titus 3:4–5 NIV)

Did you notice those wonderful attributes of God toward sinful man? "Kindness," "love," and "mercy."

Saved by Grace

How different the degree of assurance that comes from a life of faith in God's salvation rather than our works. The Bible gives the clearest of assurance when it says, "Therefore, there is now no condemnation for those in Christ Jesus" (Romans 8:1). Where does that assurance come from? It flows from the grace of God toward man, not the works of man toward God.

When it comes to salvation, God in His infinite wisdom designed His own grace-laden plan. Since He is perfectly sinless, God cannot allow sin nor sinful people in His holy presence. He originally created humans to commune with Him, but man violated His perfect standard by rebelling against Him.

Our original ancestors, Adam and Eve, committed that dreadful first and fatal act. As a result, every person born into the human race since that time is a sinner by nature and by choice. That sin has put an insurmountable barrier between us and God. God knew that no matter how hard humans tried, they could never acquire sinless perfection in and of themselves that would result in restored communion with Him. So, out of pure grace, He provided, at great cost to Himself, the only way this could be accomplished.

Here is how God did it: at just the right time, He sent His only and perfect Son, Jesus Christ, to live among men on this earth. As God in flesh, Jesus became fully human, yet (unlike all humans before or after Him), He never sinned. He lived a totally perfect life. He was eventually unjustly accused of sin by the very humans He came to redeem, and went to a cruel and shameful death on a cross, bearing the sins of all humanity on Himself. He became our substitute. He bore on Himself the judgment that should have been ours on account of our sin.

But then, giving proof of His divine power and personhood, He arose bodily from the grave three days after His death. He showed Himself to many over a period of forty days to give evidence of His miraculous resurrection. Following that, He ascended victoriously back into heaven, having completed His mission of conquering sin and death on behalf of man.

No, at first glance this arrangement doesn't seem to make much sense to us humans. But it is all part of God's redemptive plan on our behalf. Together with the totality of Scripture, it perfectly makes sense.

One Condition

However, there is a condition for one to be able to experience this God-given pardon for sin. Every individual must intentionally appropriate (receive) this provision of salvation. God doesn't force it upon anyone. Nor is salvation automatically applied to everyone. As God reaches out to us with this amazing gift, we must humbly accept it by faith. The Bible says, "For you are saved by grace through faith, and this is not from yourselves; it is God's gift—not from works, so that no one can boast" (Ephesians 2:8–9).

We must accept it, believe it, treasure it, and prize it as the most important possession in the world.

While polls show that most people believe that heaven and hell exist, most doubt that many people are on their way to that bad place called hell. The majority of people believe that they are heaven-bound. But the Bible plainly says something to the contrary. Jesus said in Matthew 7:13–14 (NIV):

> Enter through the narrow gate. For wide is the gate and broad is the road that leads to destruction, and many enter through it. But small is the gate and narrow the road that leads to life, and only a few find it.

Sadly, based on these words spoken by Jesus, the only conclusion is that the majority of people in the world are not going to heaven. Regretfully, they are in fact on their way to an eternity in hell. This is a very disturbing and sobering thought.

This conclusion provokes the question: Why is the heaven-bound group so small and the hell-bound crowd so large? Is it because that's the way God wants it to be? Did God set out to have only a small and exclusive "club" to commune eternally with Him and enjoy the glories of heaven? No, that's not the case. The Bible states very explicitly that He is "not willing (i.e., 'desiring') that any should perish" (2 Peter 3:9 NKJV).

Dethroning God

This may help explain: God desires that all accept His free gift of salvation. But in His omniscience, He knows the hearts of all mankind, including their motives and deepest thoughts. Men want to be God-like in that they want to control their own destinies. They want to live according to their own standards. They are rebels at heart. They want to create their own concept of heaven and hell and determine for themselves the norms of entry into each place. Consequently, they make entry into heaven so easy that they readily qualify. Conversely, they make entry into hell so restrictive that they personally never feel in danger of ending up there.

According to Matthew 25:41, hell was primarily created for rebellious angels led by Satan, who pridefully attempted to overthrow God. It is a place especially tooled for eternal torment and despair. Humans gained admittance to this destination when they, too, sinned against the holy God and then rejected His provision for redemption through Jesus. In essence, humans are no different than Satan when they dethrone God from their lives. Thus they deserve eternal separation from Him also. And the hollowness of that eternal separation in and of itself is hell enough, whether there be further torment or not.

The Bible says in the book of Revelation that at the last judgment "anyone whose name was not found recorded in the Book of Life would be thrown into the lake of fire" (20:15 NLT). It sounds brutal, but it's the plain and clear fact. Each and every one of us need to make sure to avoid eternal separation from God. Thus, the most pressing question for every person should be: "How do I make sure that my name is written in the Book of Life?"

Study Questions

1. How bad does one need to be to be sent to hell?

2. Is it possible for regular churchgoers, who profess to be Christians, to be on the wrong road?

3. Is there anything wrong with showing God's love by helping people? Do these acts alone guarantee entrance into heaven?

4. Are there other ways to heaven besides believing in Jesus Christ as one's personal Savior? How can you be sure?

5. Can people who have never had the opportunity to hear of Jesus really be on the road to hell? Is that fair?

6. How does our view of God and eternity affect future generations?

   What does Jesus say? Read Psalm 53:3; Mark 10:18; John 14:6–7; Acts 4:12.

7. Does great intelligence help or hinder the quest for spiritual truths? Why?

CHAPTER 4

The Other Side

I felt an urge to explore the opposite side of the tableland. I jetted up above the land mass and, in a short time, landed somewhere between the glowing red edge and the brilliant light at the center.

Although I was geographically in a different place, the scene seemed the same. The Road to Eternity was there, and it was separated into the same two divisions. There were the same many broad lanes leading to hell and the one narrow lane to heaven. From their dress and mannerisms, I knew these people were different from the previous ones I had spoken with. But I was not able to clearly discern who they were.

Just like the location I had visited previously, the majority of travelers had chosen the lanes to hell. These lanes were very crowded, and the people were talking about the same mundane things as those in the previous area I had visited. They spoke in different languages, which—amazingly—I could understand. As I looked closer, I could not help but notice that the road to heaven was almost void of travelers. My heart sank within me as I realized that so many were traversing the wrong road.

Ahmad

I took a close look at the throng coming down the road toward me. I could distinguish several large, distinctive groups coming my way. As the members approached, I picked out the one who was leading all the others and politely asked him who they were. I explained that I was a newly-arrived visitor to his country.

"We are members of the only true religion," he replied proudly, as we fell into pace together. Since it looked like he was going to be talkative, I asked him his name.

"I am Ahmad, imam of a local house of worship. I have been an imam for quite some time, having mastered our Prophet's teachings."

"It is an honor to speak with you, Mr. Ahmad. Since you have mastered the prescribed teachings, I am curious to know if they have anything to say about heaven and hell."

"Of course they do!" he replied "Surely you have heard of our Prophet, who was given the words directly from Allah himself about how we can achieve eternal bliss. He told us if we daily perform the prescribed ritualistic works found in our holy writings, along with others at the prescribed times, we will most likely merit paradise. Conversely, if one does not believe in the revelations of our Messenger, he will enter eternal damnation as an infidel."

"You mean to tell me that if you do all these things your Messenger instructed you to do, you still do not know for certain that you are going to make it into heaven?" I quizzed.

"Well, true followers probably do, but no one in the whole wide world can know that for sure this side of death," he responded without much enthusiasm. Then he brightened up a bit and added, "But we have two special, elite works that guarantee one's entrance. And, if we do make it to heaven, we will be rewarded with seventy virgins. Sounds pretty good, eh?" he added with zest and a playful nudge to my side.

At that remark, I glanced at the ones standing behind him, who were all dressed in black fabric, from head to toe. The only human features I could distinguish were piercing eyes looking out at me. I faintly heard a few high-pitched utterances coming from behind the cloth, so I made the deduction that they were female.

I tried to ask one of the "dark ones" if there were any special incentives for them in heaven, as there were for the men, but all I got in response were those dark eyes darting at Ahmad, then me. After a few awkward seconds, there was total disengagement as they moved away.

I looked back at Ahmad and could immediately tell that he wasn't happy with the question I had proposed to this group. He was probably also offended that I had taken the liberty to speak directly to his women. In order to calm him, I asked him if he knew who Jesus was. I knew I was successful when he crisply responded, "An outstanding and highly respected prophet whom we call Isa, and one who comes close to the status of our highly venerated Prophet—but certainly not on the same level as our great one."

When I told him that, according to the Bible, the only way to enter heaven was to trust solely in Jesus' work of redemption on one's behalf and not in one's own efforts—and that furthermore he was on the road leading to hell—his eyes caught fire, and I could see rage building in his face. For an instant I thought he was going to do me bodily harm, but in my strange condition I didn't think that was possible, so I wasn't too concerned.

"Why do you Christians insist on equating the prophet Isa with God?" he asked belligerently. "That is the ultimate blasphemy! God is so powerful and highly transcendent, no human could begin to compare to him. And he is only one who reveals himself as the One High God. Yet, you insist that the prophet Isa is Allah too. Rubbish!"

"I only ask that you not only consider His claims about being the Son of God but that you read for yourself about His works, miracles, and astounding resurrection from the dead," I said. "All these facts together—and even more—show Him to be God in flesh and Savior of the world."

"Well, that leads me to another issue I have with you Christians," retorted Ahmad. "How can you say that someone else can save you? No one can save you but yourself. That is your responsibility! You must faithfully perform the works of salvation as prescribed in our holy book in order to be accepted by Allah."

As I was about to respond, Ahmad turned quickly and stomped away. It was obvious that he was upset and the conversation had abruptly ended. I stood watching as he and his entourage continued on their way. Overwhelmed by sadness, I thought about how ineffective and possibly inappropriate my approach to Ahmad had been.

What will it take to reach into the hearts of these sincere yet misguided people? I asked myself. I fell to my knees and sincerely prayed, "Dear Lord of the harvest, please send forth workers to these needy and spiritually misguided people. Send workers who will learn and live in their language, culture, and worldview . . . workers who will build relationships and incarnate your message so that these dear people will one day believe."

After praying, I got back to my feet and looked around. Undeterred by my lack of success up to this point, I headed to another cluster of people coming down the broad road.

The Honorable Mr. Brahmin

This group didn't look as well connected to each other as the one I had just encountered. In fact, the closer I got the more obvious it was that they were hardly engaged with one another.

While they were traveling on the broad road, a small contingent was far off to the side of the broad road, as far as you could possibly get. As I tried to get close to the "side-roaders," they kept pulling away like I wasn't supposed to have any contact with them. (Could it be that my deodorant protection hadn't made the transitions?) I could see in their eyes that these people had great admiration for the ones parallel to them, yet they made no effort to join them. The majority of the group didn't even seem to notice the ones who were moving along with them. I got the notion that these two groups were never to have any contact with each other. Figuring that I wasn't going to be successful in talking to them, I moved back toward the main group.

After surveying them for a few minutes, I picked out a distinguished-looking fellow who, with turban and a long beard, appeared to be the leader. His distinctive garb set him apart from everyone else. The group of followers around him gave him deference, offering him food and other comforts.

Cautiously, I tapped him on the shoulder, gave a polite bow, and asked if I could speak to him for a few minutes. He seemed a little startled, like I had woken him from deep thought. It finally registered what I had asked, and he gently nodded his head. When I asked what I should call him, he replied that I could address him simply as Brahmin. I had never heard of anyone by that name before, but I liked it, as it sounded rather authoritative.

I decided I should be more polite and culturally sensitive this time. So I engaged him in some small talk before getting on to my most pointed question. In a friendly manner, we talked about our places of birth, our countries, our families, and even the kind of food we enjoyed most. It soon became evident that we were polar opposites in life experiences. And this would bear out in our perceptions of eternity as well. I finally asked him directly if he knew he was traveling on the road to hell.

He smiled at me and replied, "There are many paths in life, my son, that lead to many places. But I've never heard of one leading to a place called hell. Would you mind explaining that to me?"

Finally, I thought, *here is someone who seems willing to hear me out.*

As fully as I could, I explained that hell was a terrible place where one goes after he leaves this life if he doesn't believe in Jesus Christ, the Son of God, who came to make a glorious destination possible.

"So, you are saying that hell is a bad place?" he inquired

It went through my mind that this was going to be an interesting discussion because this learned man had no clue as to what I was talking about. I then proceeded to answer his question. "Mr. Brahmin, hell is a very bad place. The Bible gives several descriptions: a place of eternal fire, a place that is completely dark, a place of anguish, and a place totally without the goodness of God."

"Oh, that does sound like a very bad place," he said in horror. "And does the unfortunate one escape from this place?" he asked.

As I began to respond, the whole group did two side-steps and then continued with a normal gait. Not being privy to the dance step, I trudged straight ahead, only to hear a crunch under my foot and then a collective groan from the assembly. I received numerous hard stares and saw several people put their hands together, bow, and utter what I assumed was a prayer for the dearly departed. I had no idea as to what had just transpired. Looking at the road, the only thing I could see was a squashed bug.

"Sir, you must be more careful," Mr. Brahmin admonished. "Your carelessness has sent a soul into another existence, and he may not have been ready to go."

Still confused about the flattened insect, I pushed through the door the traveler had just opened in the conversation: "Mr. Brahmin, what do you think is going to happen to you when your life on this road is finished?" I asked.

"As you can see by my privileged position, I have almost achieved *moksa,* or 'release,' from the endless cycles of death and rebirth. I have died and been reborn many times and am now on the threshold of reaching Nirvana. If I do reach Nirvana this time, then I will achieve the end of my reincarnations and will be in eternal bliss."

"Let me make sure I have this right," I continued. "According to your belief system, you can be reborn many times, each time hoping to reach Nirvana, but you never will have any real assurance you are on the right track. You will only know for sure when you finally arrive there."

"That is correct, my son. No one can ever be sure until death. We have many, many gods in our religion. We can follow as many as we wish. But, none of them give assurance of one's future destination this side of death."

My heart was distressed to hear such uncertainty. "May I give you a very short summary of the essence of the Christian belief system?" I asked.

"Please do, my son; we are open to all ideas," he replied.

"The Bible teaches that the world was created by the one true God. Man was the special object of His creation and was created to fellowship with this loving God. God created man not as a mere puppet, but gave him free will. Man used that free will to rebel against his creator, resulting in a wide gulf between himself and God. The Bible calls that rebellion 'sin,' and every human, including you and me, is enslaved in it by nature and by choice. We can't help it because we are born into it. It is something we all, unfortunately, inherit.

"But God loved His created humans so much that He set into motion His plan to bring mankind back to Himself. He sent His only Son, Jesus, to live on the earth, and eventually let Him be tortured and killed by the very humans He loved so much. Then, showing His divine power, God raised up His Son from the dead and took Him back to heaven." I could see puzzlement on the face of Mr. Brahmin as I told the story.

"Now here's the really great part: if you acknowledge that you have sinned against God and believe that His Son, Jesus, died in your place to take care of that sin, He promises the certainty that you will go to heaven when you die. There is nothing you can do to achieve heaven; just believe and accept what God has done for you.

"And now for the really bad part: if you reject God's gift of salvation, then you can never be with Him in heaven, and therefore you will be relegated to hell—for He is a holy God, and, as such, cannot permit sin in His presence. And to be frank with you, Mr. Brahmin, whether you call what we are walking on a path or a road, it leads to eternal separation from God. It is also called the 'path to destruction.'"

Mr. Brahmin gave me a dismissive smile and said, "Well, my friend, as I said earlier, there are many paths to eternal bliss, and it sounds like you have found a good one, perfectly fit for you. I wish you well on your journey, and if you aren't successful in this life I'm sure you will get another chance in the next."

Then he added, "There are many gods, and everyone just needs to find the one that best suits him. And now I must bid you goodbye, as I have several offerings to present to the gods at the temple today." With that, he gave a courteous nod and continued down the road, looking this way and that to make sure he harmed no living thing that crossed his path.

Reflection: Can Salvation Be Found in Other Religions?

In his book *New Birth or Rebirth? Jesus Talks with Krishna*, Ravi Zacharias makes a statement that is difficult to grasp for the many who are conditioned by social pluralism. Stemming the tide against popular misconception, Zacharias asserts:

> The popular aphorism "All religions are fundamentally the same and only superficially different" simply is not true. It is more correct to say that all religions are, at best, superficially similar but fundamentally different.[7]

Clearly, all religions do not teach the same thing, especially when it comes to the core issue of salvation, which encompasses spiritual deliverance and paths to eternity. All religions are fundamentally different on this critical point.

Differences Between Religions

Although similarities are found in some of the peripheral or non-core teachings, all religions by their very nature are exclusive and thus posit an exclusive means of salvation. It simply is not true, as is popularly held, that we are all on different religious paths, but end up at the same place.

Again, Zacharias asserts that anyone who claims that all religions are the same not only shows an ignorance of religions but also a caricatured view of the best-known ones. Every religion at its core is exclusive.[8] Serious proponents of any major religion would not claim that all religious paths lead to the same final end. Yet, in the pluralistic culture in which we live, how quick is the tendency to believe that they do!

But, there is one serious matter on which all religions do agree. All maintain that mankind is entrapped in a desperate spiritual predicament. Our existence in this world is not as it should be—not even close. Humans are under a spiritual curse. And it is a mammoth spiritual problem that has caused the deep moral imperfections, inner unrest, discontent, and utter despair all of mankind experiences. There is no religion that denies this reality.

However, each religion postulates its own particular "cure" to this fundamental spiritual predicament. Put simply (and this is an abbreviated simplification), the answers to man's predicament according to major religions are as follows:

Table #1:

Religion	Predicament	Cure
Animism	Menacing spirits and ghosts	Appease the spirit world
Hinduism	Ignorance	Knowledge and discipline
Buddhism	Suffering caused by desire	8-fold path of self improvement
Islam	Self-centeredness	Submission to Allah
Judaism	Broken relationships	Harmony/maintain relationships

Notice that there is an element of truth from each religion as to what man's spiritual predicament is. However, each only touches on and addresses the symptoms of sin rather than the underlying disease itself. Scriptures make it clear that *sin* is man's root spiritual problem. Sin is the root cause of all other spiritual symptoms. The symptoms identified by other religions are actually the outcomes of sin.

Man's Greatest Predicament

If we were to single out one of God's attributes as overriding all others, it would be His holiness. All of His other attributes as expressed toward man (love, justice, compassion, etc.) fall in line with (and never contradict) His holiness. It is sin, something that even a loving God cannot overlook, that separates man from God and His holy presence.

Sin is doing what is contrary to God's holy nature. Scripture presents the issue this way:

1) No person is innocent in his sin.

    "Therefore, just as sin came into the world through one man, and death through sin, and so death spread to all men because all sinned." (Romans 5:12 ESV)

2) Every person, as a sinful human being, is alienated from God because of sin.

    "And you, who once were alienated and hostile in mind, doing evil deeds, he has now reconciled in his body of flesh by his death, in order to present you holy and blameless and above reproach before him." (Colossians 1:21–22 ESV)

3) Our common sinful humanity, regardless of our religious upbringing or current affiliation, separates us from God. Therefore, His great love provided a way for man to circumvent the curse of his sin and establish a relationship with Him.

    "God is love. In this the love of God was made manifest among us, that God sent his only Son into the world, so that we might live through him. In this is love, not that we have loved God but that he loved us and sent his Son to be the propitiation for our sins." (1 John 4:8–10 ESV)

4) By His very nature, God is love, and He demonstrates His love toward mankind even in mankind's rebellious state:

    "But God shows his love for us in that while we were still sinners, Christ died for us." (Romans 5:8 ESV)

One Way

God provided that propitiation (satisfaction) be made for man's sins. Love combined with holiness demanded sacrifice. His holiness had to be satisfied, and out of love He satisfied it through the sacrifice of His Son.[9] Those who accept this gift of grace are welcomed to enjoy eternity in fellowship with Him forever.

We need to not be duped by the romantic notion that somewhere, some people by some other means have found some other legitimate path to God outside of Jesus' redemptive work. That simply is not true. The Bible teaches that it is not true. Life experience proves that it is not true. Yet, this faulty opinion continues to persist, even among Christ followers.

Just because a person is religious does not mean he is righteous in the sense that God accepts him. It is not the sincerity, frequency, or intensity of one's religious efforts that cause one to be acceptable to God. Rather it is grace alone, through faith alone, in Christ alone that brings salvation. This is a universal truth that applies to all peoples, no matter the country, culture, or religious affiliation: "For you are saved by grace through faith, and this is not from yourselves; it is God's gift—not from works, so that no one can boast" (Ephesians 2:8–9).

Assurance of Eternal Life

Resulting good works are performed in gratitude to God for the wonderful gift of salvation, not for ingratiating oneself to God. No human effort can be added to the effort God has made on behalf of man. This is the great divide between biblical Christianity and every other religion. Biblical Christianity is grace-based; all other religions are merit-based. Merit-based religions can never bring assurance that enough has been done to earn one's way into heaven. That is why there is no certainty of eternal life in other religions. One never knows if he has done enough or is all "paid up" at any given time. Thus, works must incessantly continue to be done.

The contrast with believing faith—the absence of all works—in Christ could not be more stark! Paul says it clearly and succinctly in Romans 8:1: "Therefore, there is now no condemnation for those who are in Christ Jesus" (NIV).

In closing, the relation between God and His salvation as revealed in Scripture, and assurance of salvation in contrast to all other religions, can be seen in the modified chart below:[10]

Table #2:

	The Christian Gospel	All Other Religions
How to know God	Has disclosed himself	Must be discovered
God's holiness	Upheld as being absolute	Denied, diminished or disregarded
Basis for salvation	God has completed the work of salvation on our behalf through the death of Jesus Christ	Human effort, must exert one's self to save one's self
Level of assurance of going to heaven	Absolute assurance	No assurance

Study Questions

1. Why do you suppose there are so many religions in the world?

2. If man is instinctively religious, why is he not also instinctively righteous?

3. Do you believe that there are many paths leading to the same destination, called heaven, and that the important thing is to make sure you are on one of those many optional paths?

4. How would you define sin?

5. Do you believe that man's primary spiritual predicament is sin? Why or why not? If not, what do you believe better describes man's predicament?

6. Do you have an unqualified assurance of salvation? On what do you base it?

7. Why is it that adherents of other religions do not have assurance before they die that they will enter heaven?

What does Jesus say? Read Luke 19:10; John 14:1–6.
What else does the Bible say? Read Ephesians 2:1–10.

CHAPTER 5

Crossing the Great Divide

I jetted off once again above the landmass, relieved to be leaving the other side of the world. In a relatively short time I landed back in familiar territory. I was among people who spoke my language and, for the most part, looked and acted like me. After my cross-cultural experience, I was all the more determined do a better job close to my home turf. So, I settled again on the wider of the two roads.

From my position on the broad road, I peered over to the narrower lane leading to heaven and noticed again that it was nearly void of traffic. The gap between the two was nearly imperceptible, but there definitely was a divide. Feeling depressed from my previous conversations and the lack of any consideration from the interviewees, I decided it would be advantageous to explore the broad road more thoroughly. While I couldn't see what was causing the separation, inwardly I knew that I couldn't simply cross over the barrier.

So I waited awhile until I saw two women traveling next to each other but on different sides of the divide. From my short distance away, I could tell that they were engaged in a serious conversation. I crept closer, and (trying not to be obvious that I was listening in on their discussion) I overheard the one on the hell side asking questions about Jesus. While I couldn't quite make out what she was asking, I saw that the questioner frequently paused to consider what she was being told by the other woman. The heaven-side lady seemed to be getting help with her answers from some unseen force.

I followed the pair for some distance until I saw the hell-side lady's countenance change from confusion to one of recognition of the truth. For a moment she paused and looked down, and for the first time I could see what she was seeing. The invisible barrier between the lanes was a chasm so deep and wide that its scope was immeasurable. Its immensity took my breath away. I stepped back a bit, afraid of falling in. I remembered a time in my non-hovering past, standing on the edge of the Grand Canyon and being amazed at its depth and width. But that was like a small gulley compared to this. A mist was rising from the abyss below, forming letters—the word *SIN*—which wafted through the air like they had been written by an airplane.

I could see that the changed lady was veering off the broad road and was headed to a small gate. The entryway was narrow, the gate low. Over it was written, "To get to heaven, you must take this Cross-over. This is the only entry point!"

The Constricted Crossing

I noticed that to enter the narrow gate, a person was forced to kneel down to get rid of the baggage that they were carrying on their back. It was evident that, to move forward, a traveler had to move on hands and knees. All the things that a person had accumulated through their lifetime, things that they thought would bring them eternal life and happiness, had to be discarded.

Several people were obviously very rich, considering the large loads they were transporting. People stood by the gate looking confused. Over the years, they had accrued so much "stuff" that they were having a tough time throwing it all away. A few who were wanting to "Cross over" couldn't force themselves to abandon things like family, career, and self-importance, and therefore couldn't fit through the narrow gate—and so they became stuck. The few who made it across were able to thrust aside or deflate the things they were carrying so they did not hinder their entry.

There were also some D-workers nearby who were using bullhorns to belt out to those who happened to stop, "Ignore this gate and sign; there is a much easier crossing down the road!" A few were handing out blinders that reminded me of ones fitted on racehorses. Some of the travelers seemed relieved to hear that there was an alternative crossing. Others ridiculed the few who had cast off their burdens and knelt in order to go through the constricting gate.

As I peeked over the edge of the great chasm, I could see scattered among the rocks on the chasm walls the remains of unsuccessful attempts to bridge the wide gap. Ruined structures were in abundance. There were many types of designs, but they all had one thing in common: not one had come close to bridging the wide divide. There were piles of "Good Works," "Self Sacrifices," "Eastern Religious Beliefs," "Super-Intelligence," "Self-Reliance," and many other structures scattered among the debris. I even saw many ruined structures labeled "False and Watered-down Christian Beliefs."

It was obvious that humans had all failed in their attempts to reach the other side. I wondered what had become of the well-intentioned engineers. Stacked by the low, narrow gate were the personal belongings of the ones who had "Crossed over." Onlookers on the broad road were in disbelief that such valuable possessions and long-held views could be discarded as if they were worthless.

I glanced at the now radiant lady as she gingerly began her journey across the chasm. A rugged cross appeared to lie across the wide gulf, spanning the distance. It was stained red with what I assumed was dried blood. At the entrance, the woman went down to her knees and began to crawl across the wide gap on that cross. She was hesitant at first, but as she continued she grew more and more confident. Before she reached the other side, she got up and almost ran with delight!

I heard a great shout of joy that seemed to come from heaven itself. The two ladies joyfully embraced, and then continued down the narrow road together, along with other pilgrims. As I looked as the two ladies' faces, I could tell that even though they had traveled much of life together, now, for the first time, they were truly on the same road. As I glanced around this greatest of canyons, I realized that what held me in awe and amazement was not the deep, long chasm but the way across it. I wondered how such a horrible but simple structure could put to shame all the futile man-made constructions strewed around it.

Glimpse of Eternity

I followed the lady who had just switched lanes and watched as she suddenly sped up, leaving her friend far behind. Somehow I was able to follow her, and (in what seemed like a short time) we arrived at the same bright, warm light that I had seen at the center of the table during my hovering. The lady completely disappeared into that mysterious Radiance. As I moved closer, I found myself on my knees, longing to continue the journey with her, to go deeper into that glorious Illumination. But try as I might, I could make no progress. I began begging for permission to be let in. With my whole being, I began shouting, "Glory to God in the highest!" But I heard only a soft voice whisper, "Not yet."

Demon Deception

With great disappointment, I returned to the heaven road and was surprised to see some of the D workers moving along with the few travelers on this narrow path. *What are they doing on this side?* I wondered. Considering what I had previously seen, it didn't seem like they should be on this street at all. Unnoticed, I maneuvered closer to one who was walking near one the heaven-bounders. Most of the time, the Ds were silent, but every so often one would say something softly into the ear of a heaven-bounder. From what I could tell, the victim couldn't see who was making the suggestions. It took awhile to train my ear to hear what this particular D was saying, but through intense concentration and lip-reading, I finally was able to pick up his words.

"Look over there, to the other road. Aren't they having a good time? What would it hurt to join them for a while? And look at that smooth surface. It sure would be easier traveling over there with all your friends than here, wouldn't it? This road is rocky and so narrow, you might get hurt if you stay on it."

Other crafty attackers were implanting other subtle thoughts, such as "You really don't have to go to church to worship God," or "Some of the Bible is true, but other parts are obvious exaggerations."

Without waiting for a response, the Ds would back off, letting the words float around in their victims' heads without any debate.

I overheard one of the Ds whisper to another imp, "You know, there is no way we can force this person off this road. We haven't been given the power to do so. Our only hope is that, over time, he will gradually leave on his own or just drift away. Be careful, but keep working on him."

After each thought implantation, the D would give his charge's shoulder a gentle nudge toward the parallel, wider road. The heaven-bounder didn't seem to notice that he was gradually moving off his intended path and closer to the one that the masses of humanity were traveling.

I noticed that the heaven road looked nothing like its counterpart. Besides being narrow, it was full of ups and downs and obstacles that either had to be pushed aside or traversed with a great deal of effort. When a person was dealing with these obstructions, a D would take the opportunity to whisper in an ear, "Maybe it would be easier on the other road."

Sometimes an alert fellow traveler would caution a friend to beware of the Ds and their distorted messages. When that happened, a D would softly say to its fertile target, "Ds don't really exist—they are just an antiquated idea from the mythological past." I noticed a thin smile on the face of the D after he used what must have been his favorite line.

I struck up several conversations with those on the narrow path. Most of these people were confident about where they were heading and seemed content (although surprisingly unexcited) about their final destination. They explained that while they were waiting for their personal road to end, they felt a great responsibility to tell as many as they could about their great find: the Cross-over.

My visit on this road did not last nearly as long as I would have liked. Frustration doesn't begin to describe how I felt as I was again pulled up and away and back to my suspended state by some unseen force.

Fast Movers

As I hovered above the mass of humanity below, I sensed that my time was running short and I needed to move along more quickly if I was to grasp the full meaning of what was happening below. So far, it hadn't made any difference where I landed; the results had been pretty much (and disappointingly) the same. So I selected a sector where I didn't think I had been before and zoomed into the midst of it.

At this location, I noticed an additional outside lane. It was like the moving walkways I had seen at airports. This one was raised a bit, about a foot higher than the rest of the road. There were breaks every once in awhile where people could get off and on. At those breaks there were signs that read,

> "Reserved for the Rich, Powerful, Athletic, Intellectual, and Beautiful ... and for people who think they are."

Ignoring the qualifications, I hopped on, right away I saw that it took little to no effort to move along this section of the Road to Eternity. This lane wasn't as crowded as the others, and most of the people had an air of confidence that they were headed in the right direction.

I noticed that more guys wearing the D ball caps were at the breaks of the walkway, helping distinguished people to get on. They were giving everyone pats on the back, encouraging words, and a complementary drink as they performed their work. They became very agitated on the rare occasions when one of the elites tried to get off, doing everything they could to keep them in the fast lane. Their best technique to keep everyone aboard was to surround the escapees with their friends who dumped bucket of ridicule on them. It worked almost every time.

I tried to ask several travelers if they knew that they were on the road to hell. One guy, who was a little portly, thought my question was a big joke and remarked that at least all his friends were going there too! With his hand raised and clenching his drink, he shouted, "Party on!" and disappeared into the crowd. Maybe one of the strangest sights of all was that a few of these "special people" were sitting in large hand-woven baskets, oblivious to the fact that they were advancing toward their destination. I had no idea what that was all about and chose to ignore it.

As we moved along, the people who were walking below and beside us looked up with admiration and some envy. Sometimes they would break out with a rousing cheer when they saw someone popular whom they recognized. You could tell that these elevated souls enjoyed the adoration they received from the more lowly, and that they inwardly felt they deserved it. Some would wave back or give a more dignified nod, acknowledging the adulation. Some of the more ambitious lower-level people ran alongside, trying to keep up with this exclusive group. But most gave up after awhile and resumed their normal pace.

When we arrived at the small breaks in the walkway, some of the lower-level travelers who had managed to keep up would jump on and let out an excited yell, as if they had won a grand prize. They looked around, amazed at how easy the travel was and delighted to be in the elite company they were now keeping. Sadly, they were even less aware of the signs that passed by, almost in a blur:

> "YOU ARE ON THE WRONG SIDE. YOU
> ARE ON THE FAST ROAD TO HELL."

They were so caught up in their achievements and new status that the signs meant nothing to them and seemed to be absolutely ridiculous. Those who were already on this fast track didn't seem excited to be joined by the newcomers. They generally tried to ignore them.

E's

From my new position on the conveyor with the lofty ones, I could see another group of people I hadn't noticed before. They were on the narrow road but were engaging people across the invisible barrier on the broad road. This small group had two divisions; one was distinguishable because they each wore a dark suit with a tie with a large embroidered E in the middle. Each was carrying a large black book that took two hands to carry and looked quite heavy.

The other group was dressed in expensive jeans and brightly-colored tee shirts with a small "E" over their hearts. On the back of the shirts was the word "heaven" with a small box next to it and a check mark in the square. Below that was the word "hell," accompanied by a similar small box with a sad face in it. Instead of carrying big books, in their hands they held the latest smartphone that included a black book app. Both groups of evangelists were actively engaged in talking to people on the road, and seemed to be genuinely concerned about the direction in which the travelers were headed.

I noticed that both groups used several different techniques to connect with people. Some of the dark suits would hit the big black books they were carrying with the palms of their hands, creating a thumping sound as they talked. One dark-suiter was whacking an unsuspecting person over the head with the big book as he emphasized a point.

The tee-shirters put their arms around people's shoulders and held out the smartphone for them to look at. As they moved their fingers around on the screen, words and images that they used in their conversations appeared. Sometimes they held the phone up to the ear of whomever they were engaged with so the traveler could hear a recording artist singing.

Both groups had a few successful encounters. But mostly they were ignored by the masses as they traveled down the road. In fact, the E's were almost trampled when they knelt and prayed with new heaven-bounders.

Several times I noticed the D's and the E's were involved with the same person. While the E was face to face with a person, explaining his point, the D was behind him, whispering is his ear. It didn't look like the E was aware of what was happening, and certainly the person being talked to wasn't.

Out of the corner of my eye I detected an especially energetic E tee-shirter running alongside the fast-movers. He was shouting to the elevated ones a warning of the consequences of staying on the road they were on. A fellow, whom the other people called G.M. Smart, shouted a reply to the nearly exhausted E person: "Can't you see that we are special? We are special because of our superior knowledge and abilities. We don't need made-up gods to please or superstitions to find meaning. We are gods to ourselves, and we have no use for your unsophisticated, primal beliefs." Others in the fast-moving group nodded in approval, partying on with their fast-moving friends.

Distractions

Rarely did it happen (in fact I saw it only once) that one of the elevated ones got off the walkway and veered onto the heaven lane. When that occurred, the D ball cappers tried everything possible to bring them back before they accessed the Cross-over that bridged the great divide. The Ds would offer them more of what they already had. When that strategy didn't work, they moved beside them and appealed to their intellect with questions about God, hoping to bring them to doubt. Sometimes they created a massive diversion in the person's life so they would stop thinking about the narrow lane.

But I noticed that the imps didn't do this to only the fast-movers. They worked on anyone who came close to the heaven lane. They were uncanny in their effectiveness. But once the Cross-over appeared for someone to make the passage, the D's would shrink away in fear. They couldn't stand to look at it. They seemed to know it was the emblem of their ultimate doom.

Reflection: Does a Loving God Send People to Hell?

Non-believers often ask this question to defend why they don't believe in God or hell. This question even stumps some Christians. This question is not usually asked with the intent of seeking a thoughtful answer, but as a way of ending all discussion about hell itself. The question also shows a lack of understanding as to the nature of God and His provision of salvation for mankind.

Discussion of this topic must begin on the premise that God is absolutely perfect. In His perfection, He created everything with perfection as well. It follows that when God created humans, He created them in a state of perfection, too. He created them with the ultimate purpose of communing with Him and enjoying Him forever. But He did not create them to be, as C.S. Lewis pointed out, "marionettes."[11]

God gave man a free will so that when we worship Him, it comes from the heart, not through a robotic response. None of us want our family and friends to love us by force. We don't want them to be like the doll that, when pushed in the right spot, exclaims, "I love you!" We don't desire forced love, and neither does God.

When we sin, we throw into place a barrier that prohibits communion with God, and we know it. We feel it in our inner being. We feel dirty in the presence of holiness. We feel ashamed and disgusted with ourselves, and we know that God is not pleased with us either.

That is why after Adam and Eve sinned, they hid themselves when God showed up to commune with them. And every human being ever since has dodged God because of his or her sin. We instinctively know that, because of our sin, we cannot stand in His holy presence. From time immemorial, man has tried to bridge that gap of imperfection with his own imperfect efforts. But that does not work. All efforts, no matter by whom, how intense, or how oft-repeated, are to no avail.

Reason for Hell

What was God's response when His perfect plan of communing with His creatures was rejected? His first response was wrath! When His first created beings, a fairly large contingent of angels, rebelled against Him, He had no choice but to cast them out of His holy presence. He created hell, a place of judgment, as their destination because of their rebellion. They were not given any opportunity for reprieve. The Bible says that they will eventually be thrown into the lake of fire, where they will dwell in torment for eternity.

Humans are no less rebellious and, according to the Bible, are headed to that same fate. The reason is quite simple: God cannot tolerate sin and rebellion in His holy presence. The condition of the human heart condemns mankind to an eternity in hell.

Throughout the Old Testament, God repeatedly demonstrated His attribute of justice. When He created mankind, He ingrained in all of us that same attribute. We humans want to see justice served, and strive to see it manifested in every area of life. We establish court systems to see it served. We build penal systems to facilitate what the courts rule. We desire to see the guilty punished for their wrongdoing and cry foul if it is not carried out. We want to see justice served.

When God's chosen people, the Israelites, consistently rejected His moral standards, in justice He allowed them to suffer the consequences of their sin. But He also kept showing His love for them by trying to restore them to Himself. However, they weren't any different than you and me in that His overtures of mercy were rejected time and again. Like the Israelites of old, we deserve God's holy wrath, just as our children deserve punishment when they disobey us as parents. Even though we sin against Him, God's desire is to restore us to fellowship, just as we desire to do so with our own children. In Ezekiel 33, God pleads for His beloved people: "As surely as I live, declares the Sovereign Lord, I take no pleasure in the death of the wicked, but rather that they turn from their ways and live. Turn! Turn from your evil ways! Why will you die?" (v. 11 NIV).

The second divine response to man's rebellion was the introduction of God's perfect salvation plan on man's behalf. This entailed extending His grace to us by sending His Son, Jesus Christ, to earth to take the sins of all humanity upon Himself. Christ suffered the consequences of our sins by His sacrificial and vicarious death on the cross on our behalf. Then, to prove that He was truly God, He rose victoriously from the grave.

All that is left for us humans to do is admit that we are sinners, intentionally turn from those sins, and believe that Jesus' provision for those sins restores us to a right relationship with God. We must acknowledge that we can never reach God through our own efforts and humbly accept the fact that the sacrifice of Jesus is the bridge over the gulf that spans the distance between us and God. By placing our faith in Jesus' sinless life, His substitutionary death, and His victorious resurrection on our behalf, we can be saved from God's judgment. And the beauty of our accepting this gracious gift is that we are rescued not only from our sin-filled ways in this life but also from the wrath of God in the next.

Man didn't dream up this grace-filled solution of bridging the gap between himself and God. This was a God-initiated rescue plan. To many, it's inconceivable that this way of grace is enough to satisfy God—it just sounds too simple. However, God in His perfect wisdom provided such a way. There is a high cost for rejecting His offer of salvation. That cost is eternal separation from God in a place the Bible explicitly calls "hell."

God and Love

People are right when they say that a loving God would never send anyone to hell. That statement is true, and the Scriptures bear it out. The most recognized verse of the Bible plainly says that, on the basis of love, God provided a way of salvation for all mankind. John 3:16 says, "For God so loved the world that he gave his one and only Son, that whoever believes in him shall not perish but have eternal life" (NIV).

Out of deep compassion for humanity, God provided the way for us to experience eternal life with Him. But this is love on His terms, not ours. This cannot be stated any clearer than through the words of the Apostle John as he reflected on the life and death of Jesus:

> This is how God showed his love among us: He sent his one and only Son into the world that we might live thorough him. This is love: not that we loved God,

but that he loved us and sent his Son as an atoning sacrifice for our sins. (1 John 4:9–10 NIV)

Incredibly, most people choose to ignore God's loving plan. They make their choice in various ways. Some reject the notion that Jesus' death was enough to bridge the sin gap. They reject the thought that God has any control over their lives at all. Others think so highly of their own abilities hat they are convinced they are gods to themselves. Still others believe they can follow their own customized plan, a plan better than God's. They believe it will yield the same result—entry into heaven and the avoidance of hell. Little do any of these people realize that rejection of His rescue plan is an affront to God.

Try to imagine for a moment that the president of the United States has invited you to a White House reception. When you arrive, he greets you with a large smile and announces that he has cashed in his most prized possession and has used the proceeds to buy you a wonderful gift. Now, imagine the president's utter dismay and even anger if you were to respond, "Thank you, Mr. President, I appreciate the thought. But I am self-sufficient and don't really want or need what you have to offer."

With that, you turn your back on the most powerful man on earth and walk away, leaving his wonderful gift in his hand. Now think about it: Would anyone be so rude? Of course not!

God is eminently more majestic than the leader of any nation. His gift of His Son to us is infinitely more valuable than any other. Yet many have the audacity to outright reject it. God knows the eternal value of His gift and the dire consequences that await those who reject it. But what is amazing is that He keeps calling to sinners, in spite of turned shoulders and hardened hearts, pleading for them to come back to Him. He persistently offers His gift in the hope that man will come to his senses and accept it. This is made clear in 2 Peter 3: "The Lord . . . is patient with you, not wanting any to perish but all to come to repentance" (v. 9).

Does this sound like the kind of Being who is so unloving and so vengeful that He celebrates the eternal ruin of those who reject Him?

Summary

Now, to give the short answer to the question at the beginning; Yes, we do have a loving God who wants us to experience His best and has provided a way for us to enjoy eternal life with Him in heaven. And no, He doesn't send anyone to hell. People send themselves there through their rebellious sin. He allows mankind to choose their final destination by their own free will.

Study Questions

1. What are some behaviors that many people believe will gain them entrance into heaven?

2. Why is the cross the only way to bridge the canyon between God and man?

3. What might be some false and watered-down Christian beliefs that fail to bridge the sin gap?

4. Why do you think the "fast-movers" are less likely to change roads?

5. In your opinion, do D's (demons) really exist? What evidence do you have that they exert their will on people? What is their present role?

6. Can you think of three people with whom you are close and who you believe, based on this chapter, are in danger of heading to hell?

7. Rich people can be on the road to heaven, but does wealth have any bearing on one's final destination?

What does Jesus say? Read Matthew 4:1–10; 19:23–26.
What else does the Bible say? Read 1 Timothy 6:9.

CHAPTER 6

Confused and Refused

One thing I hadn't noticed before was that, with some effort, the heaven-bounders could move throughout the hell-bound lanes. As long as they maintained the goal of showing the hell-bounders the way across the great divide to safety, they were all right. The chasm was still there, but to the casual observer it was indistinguishable. The heaven-bounders were aware of it and respected it. However, the hell-bounders didn't seem to have a clue that it existed.

Unfortunately, some heaven-bounders were blinded by the grandiose lifestyle of the elevated walkway and failed to remember why they were there. Sadly, a few became so intertwined with the masses on the broad road that they gradually forgot about the cross by which they had traversed the chasm. The distinction between their lifestyles and those of the people they had come to warn became increasingly vague. I wondered if my perception had been wrong and they had never really made the initial crossover like I thought they had. Did they continue on the wrong road to the very end? I don't know the answer to that. I was unable to observe them long enough to know how they ended up.

In front of me was a large group that straddled both the hell and heaven lanes. The vast majority were on the heaven side, but there were a few walking down the wide road. I quickly learned that I was in the midst of an annual convention of a conservative Christian denomination and that they were talking about the road to hell. *Now this is refreshing,* I thought. *Finally!—a group that has genuine concern about the broad road leading to destruction.*

But as I listened in, I soon became disappointed. The debate wasn't over the existence and horrors of that awful place but how much they should talk about. The prevailing idea was that they should mention it once in a while but not overdo it. Various people argued that scaring people into heaven didn't work very well. I saw a lot of head nodding and heard many "amens" in agreement from the theologians and scholars in their midst. A few dissenters brought up that Jonathan Edwards' famous sermon, "Sinners in the Hands of an Angry God," seemed to have been pretty effective and had some long-term effects. *That was a different time—people today wouldn't respond very well*, was the general consensus of the group.

A young pastor by the name of I.M. Relevant admitted that he and others like him had never preached on the topic of hell. Their congregations were full of young couples who were new at seeking God, and throwing the concept of hell at them would certainly scare them away. Besides, the topic didn't fit very well with their music emphasis. They couldn't think of one song by a contemporary Christian artist that described the awfulness of hell. In fact, they couldn't find one who even mentioned it.

A motion was made to appoint a committee to study the effects of preaching on hell to the congregations and how often it should be done. The committee was charged to do their work and report back in two years. That arrangement seemed to settle the issue for most of the group. They needed to move on to more important topics, such as how much technology should be used in their worship and what style of music was going to bring in the most people. A few debated the latest techniques in outreach.

A keynote speaker proclaimed that if the clergy were to get people to change lanes on the Road to Eternity, they needed to be more involved with them. Again, I heard quite a few loud "amens" in agreement.

I moved close to one of the Amen-ers. I read his large, gold nametag: Dr. P.T. Word. I asked him how he was going to convince people to change lanes. P.T. looked at me and, with a bit of irritation in his voice, he responded, "Son, my responsibility is to make sure the

Word of God was preached every Sunday. This is a full-time effort, and I take it very seriously."

He also noted that it was the job of his minister of evangelism and the people of his congregation to find lost people and bring them to the services. With another loud "amen" in response to something that was said up front, he moved deeper into the throng so I couldn't bother him with more "stupid" questions.

A young person who had been listening to my conversation with Dr. Word approached me and said, "It's tough for preachers like Dr. Word to have contact with the lost. Their big churches keep them very busy with meetings and conferences. Many of their kids are either in private Christian schools or home-schooled. The only interaction they have with their neighbors is when they wave to them as they pull into their garages before they push the button that lowers the door. And most of their friends and golf partners are fellow preachers. About the only regular contact they have with outsiders is with the girl with the tinny voice at the drive-through as they pick up their morning lattes. They expect the lost to come to them."

He seemed to know what he was talking about, so I left it at that.

As I felt myself being pulled upward, I wondered: *If the clergy are so reluctant to talk about hell, then how is their record on preaching about heaven?*

Reflection: If Hell Is Real,
Why Don't Preachers Talk More About It?

How many sermons have you heard on the topic of hell over the last two or three years? How about the last ten? If you're a typical parishioner, your answer is likely "none." In fact, you may be hard-pressed to remember any in the last twenty years. Preachers are no more apt to talk about the horrors of hell than the average church attendee is. In fact, many preachers may be unwilling because they perceive that such a topic could be a threat to their employment, or at the very least a hindrance for someone who is considering joining their congregation.

Some are reluctant because they don't want to be branded "that hell-fire damnation preacher who gets people all worked up." But it seems that most reluctance about preaching on hell is rooted in the fact that many aren't sure what they believe about it. Like C.S. Lewis said, being sent to hell for eternity for sins committed during a short lifetime doesn't fit the concept of a loving God. Lewis concluded, however, that we have no choice but to believe in hell because of the abundance of Scripture on it.[12]

Alternatives to Hell?

Throughout history, many theologians have tried to come up with an alternative that better fits their belief systems. Some have come to believe that after an appropriate period of time, souls in hell are simply extinguished (annihilationism). Some believe that hell has never existed and the Scriptures are simply wrong on the matter. Others take the position that after a period of time, a sufferer in hell will have served his time and will be released into heaven (a form of universalism mixed with a belief in purgatory).

While these views are becoming more popular, even the oft anti-evangelical *Time Magazine* perceived the danger of this teaching. The April 14, 2011 edition stated:

> To take away hell is to leave the church without its
> most powerful sanction. If heaven, however defined,

is everyone's ultimate destination in any event, then what's the incentive to confess Jesus as Lord in this life? In other words, if Gandhi is in heaven, then why bother with accepting Christ? If you say the Bible doesn't really say what a lot of people have said it says, then where does that stop? If the verses about hell and judgment aren't literal, then what about the ones on adultery or homosexuality? Taken to their logical conclusions, such questions could undermine much of conservative Christianity.[13]

Dr. Albert Mohler Jr., President of The Southern Baptist Theological Seminary, responds to such teaching by stating:

> We dare not retreat from all the Bible says about hell. We must never confuse the Gospel, nor offer suggestions that there may be any way of salvation outside of conscious faith in Jesus Christ. We must never believe that we can do a public relations job on the Gospel or on the character of God. We must never be unclear and subversively suggestive about what the Bible teaches.[14]

Boldness to Preach

Peter Cartwright, a nineteenth-century preacher, was an uncompromising man. One Sunday morning when he was about to preach, he was told that President Andrew Jackson was in the congregation. He was warned not to say anything out of line. When Cartwright stood to preach, he said, "I understand that Andrew Jackson is here. I have been requested to be guarded in my remarks. Andrew Jackson will go to hell if he doesn't repent!"

The congregation was in shock! How would the president respond? After services, President Jackson shook hands with Cartwright and said, "Sir, if I had a regiment of men like you, I could conquer the world."[15]

While in today's world we have little room or a bold preacher like Cartwright, our pulpits desperately need men who are not afraid to preach the whole counsel of God. Every New Testament writer talks about hell in some form. It's a subject that can't be and shouldn't be ignored.

Ligon Duncan lays out a seven-step approach on how pastors can broach the topic of hell. Among other helpful instructions, he writes:

> So also with hell, the minister's willingness to break silence and speak directly to hidden fears and questions, lovingly and carefully to be sure, but with manliness and conviction, can breed a certain receptivity, and even confidence in his words, in his audience. Speaking to the matter from the vantage point of strength and kindness enables the minister to address the subject comprehensively, probing into areas where an emotional knee-jerk reaction might otherwise function as an effective prophylactic against the truth of God's word.[16]

Given the seriousness of the matter, the topic of hell cannot be avoided. As uncomfortable as it is, pastors and Bible teachers must be willing to preach the whole counsel of God, including the reality of hell. Believers in the pew have a responsibility as well. They are tasked with holding their pastor-teachers responsible, including in regard to teaching in this area. They are also responsible to be willing to listen to difficult teaching such as this one. No one gets a pass when it comes to the responsibility of holding to and proclaiming the biblical truth about mankind's final destinations.

Study Questions

1. In your opinion, can people who are on the "heaven road" change direction and end up permanently on the "hell road"?

2. Do you know someone who appears to have done this very thing? How do they show it?

3. How long do you believe a person in hell will remain there? On what basis?

4. In your opinion, why don't evangelical preachers preach more on the topic of hell?

5. Think back to your own experiences. When was the last time you heard a sermon primarily focused on the topic of hell?

6. How often do you think preachers should mention hell?

7. If we should talk about hell as being a very frightful place that is to be avoided at all costs, what would be appropriate language to bring into that conversation?

What does the Bible say? Read 2 Peter 3:17; Revelation 20:15.

CHAPTER 7

The Narrow Road

Once more I felt myself being pulled upward, and a moment later downward again to the round, flat tableland below me. I cringed a bit as I approached the surface, fearful of a violent crash landing. But like all the other times, I was deposited softly in the middle of a road. Since I had been here briefly before, it didn't take long to realize that I was not on the broad road, but on the much narrower, less-traveled, and sometimes rocky road to heaven itself! With no one in sight, I decided to lean against a large rock and wait for the next travelers to come along.

I waited longer than I expected, but eventually I saw a group approaching. Judging from the lack of audible noise coming from this group, they were a somber bunch, and I wondered why this was so. I maneuvered myself into their midst, trying to assess them before entering into direct conversation. While they were certainly on the right road and headed in the right direction, they surprisingly didn't seem too excited about it. None seemed to notice or care about my presence, and, frustratingly, no one tried to engage me in conversation.

Finally, unable to stand the silent treatment any longer, I bellowed to no one in particular, "Do any of you know what road you're on?" I got several stares from those around me. Finally, one of the males asked, "May I help you, sir?"

"Yes," I said in a softer voice, "I have an assignment to find out about this road that you and your group are on and why people like you are here. Do you have a moment to talk?"

"Well, I guess that would be all right," he responded hesitantly. "My name is P.D. Nation, and I am one of the elders in this congregation. People call me P.D., but just to let you know, we don't usually talk about this kind of thing to strangers."

"Oh, really? Would you mind telling me why?" I inquired, trying to be agreeable as we moved on down the road.

"Well, first of all," began P.D., "we have found that most non-believers don't react well when we tell them we are on the road to heaven and they're not."

"But doesn't that give you opportunity to explain how they can get on this road too?" I quizzed.

Mr. Nation's shoulders drooped a bit as he looked at me and said, "That's just the point. The Bible says that 'few will be chosen,' so if they're not already on this road, they probably never will be. Besides, it's not up to us to save people from hell; that's God's work."

This stumped me a bit, so—in order to make things clearer—I inquired, "So let me get this straight. Since you don't know who is going to end up in heaven, you don't believe you have any responsibility to help other people get there?"

"That's essentially correct," affirmed P.D. "Everything is predestined."

That line of reasoning was confusing to me, so I changed the question. "Can you explain to me how knowing that you are going to heaven when you die affects how you live your life here on earth?"

Mr. Nation responded, "We live a pretty quiet life, trying to please God and fellowshipping with like-minded people. We try not to get caught up with the distractions of this world." The answer didn't take as long as I had expected, but, not to be deterred, I continued in my inquiry.

"May I ask you one last question?" P.D. nodded his head and seemed relieved that this inquisition would soon be coming to an end. "What do you believe heaven—your final and eternal destination—is going to be like?"

"The Bible plainly says that we are going to do a lot of praising God there, and that's good enough for me," stated Mr. Nation emphatically.

I heard one of the teenagers next to him mutter, "Sounds pretty boring to me."

This brought a quick look of reproach from P.D., but it wasn't enough to stop the teenager's friend from chipping in, "I hope Rev. Long isn't in the pulpit. His sermons already seem to go on for eternity."

This prompted a few restrained snickers from the other young people in the group. With that, P.D. grabbed the first boy and gave him a little shove forward while saying something to the effect that maybe he was on the wrong road after all.

I exited the group and waited to talk to someone else, hoping it wouldn't be too long before they came along. After some time, I saw an older couple traveling down the narrow passageway. Along with them were a number of younger people of various ages. By the way the couple shuffled along, it was evident that life had been difficult on this road, yet they seemed to take each step with a sense of purpose. Like everyone else I had met on either road, their pace suggested that there was no stopping to chat, so I fell in beside them.

I introduced myself as someone who was curious about how they came to be on this path. They seemed happy to talk and told me their names were Bee and Ever Faithful. They explained that the young people behind them were part of the family. With a quick glance behind them, I noticed that the younger ones didn't bear much physical resemblance to this couple; in fact, several looked quite different.

The couple beamed as they told me how they had crossed the great divide many years ago. She had been a child of eight, and he had been a young adult. Ever relayed that he had developed a serious interest in Bee, and she let him know that she wasn't interested in him unless he had a relationship with Jesus Christ. Bee held his arm with both hands and looked into his face as Ever related how he had never given much thought to spiritual things until Bee made him confront his spiritual "lostness." After a time of studying, and even without Bee's prodding, he knew he wanted to become a believer in Christ.

I asked the Faithfuls how knowing that they were on the narrow road to heaven had affected their lives over the years. Bee looked at me and told me that even though they were Christians, life had not been easy for them. Their first child, a son, had died shortly after birth, and their only other child, a girl, had been killed as a teenager in an automobile accident caused by a drunk driver. Ever's arm slid around his wife's waist tenderly as she continued their story.

"The only thing that got us through it," she said, "was knowing that Christ loved us and His gift of heaven would enable us to meet Him and our children once again. We also realized that since our natural children were being taken care of, we should help other children reach heaven, too. So, over the years, we have taken into our home more than twenty foster children."

Ever interjected, "God has given Bee the gift of compassion for children. We also determined early on that our goal was not only to care for the children's needs in this life, but—even more importantly— to direct them to Jesus so that their eternal lives in heaven would be secured."

Before I could ask the obvious question, Bee broke in, "We wish we could say that all the children have become Christians, but we are still praying a few into the Kingdom."

"You talk about heaven being so important to you, so—if you don't mind—tell me what you think it will be like," I said. "I talked to several people just ahead of you on this road, and, while they are glad they are going there instead of hell, they don't think heaven is going to be that enjoyable."

Bee looked at me in astonishment. "Oh, I don't know how any Christian could think that!" she said emphatically. "The Bible says we are created in God's image, so to me that means that all the things we enjoy are pieces of God. We were created to be happy, and that doesn't stop when we get to heaven. I think that all the things we enjoy here on earth will be magnified in heaven. I'm sure we will have a grand time worshiping God in person, with the best singing. Even I will be able to carry a tune!"

"Preach it," said Ever heartily, prompting Bee to prod him playfully in the side with her elbow. "But I don't think that's all we'll be doing," she continued. "I'm not only looking forward to praising God and seeing my children, my parents, and other loved ones, but I'm also looking forward to meeting new friends who have lived in the past and hearing about their lives on earth and how they came to Christ.

You know how great family reunions can be?" I nodded in agreement. "Well, this one will be much, much better."

Ever chipped in, "I'm looking forward to getting rid of this creaking old body and trading it in on the new one the Lord has prepared for me. No more sore joints, eyes that need glasses, ears that ring . . . and when I go to—" He caught himself and said, "I guess I'm getting carried away. Let's just say I'm looking forward to having a body that works right, like God designed."

Bee just shook her head as Ever continued. "The Bible reveals that God will create a New Heaven and a New Earth. So no, I don't think heaven could ever be boring. I think it will be like a theme park, but even better. Worshiping God will be our major activity, and rightfully so, but I'm sure there will be a lot of other joyful things going on. We're going to be worn out trying to enjoy everything that's available!

I noticed that both Bee and Ever kept glancing at the broad road that, as usual, was teeming with people. Ever continued, "Our hearts break when we see the people over there and know what their final destination is going to be. Many of those people are our friends and neighbors, and, as we just said, a few are the very children we have raised.

"If only someone could tell them, maybe they would cross over," he lamented.

I noticed that Ever's pace had increased while he was talking. Bee and I and the rest of the crew were having a difficult time keeping up with him. I heard him faintly say, "I see it now! What a beautiful place! I love you, Bee!" And then he was gone.

In the distance, the glowing mass to where we were headed seemed to sustain a quick "power surge" and then returned to normal. I turned to Bee to see tears flowing down her cheeks. As I tried to think of something comforting to say, I heard her mutter, "Thank You, Jesus, for taking him home. Tell him I'll be coming along shortly."

Without saying anything more to me, or even giving me another glance, she continued on, shuffling down the narrow road, with her brood following behind.

Reflection: Will Heaven Be Boring?

Heaven is that final destination where most people believe they will end up after they die. Plenty of jokes have been told about entering through the "pearly gates" and who is standing there to greet people upon arrival. You have probably told some yourself. But seriously, countless books have been written on heaven, speculating about what our existence there will be like. The Bible gives only a tantalizing peek into the details. We wish for more to satisfy our natural curiosity. However, it must be remembered that the Scripture's intent is to direct our focus toward the God of heaven rather than heaven itself. Humanly speaking, the Scriptures do not provide enough detailed information to assuage our thirst for more, and, if we're honest, quell anxiety about what our existence there will be like.

Many Christians seem to harbor some underlying apprehension about what they will do for all eternity. After all, eternity is a really, really long time! So what *do* we know about this place that God has specially prepared for those who love Him? Actually, we know enough to give us a satisfying glimpse. Seven attributes stand out.

Seven Attributes of Heaven

First of all, since God created heaven for Himself and the angels who minister to Him, we can infer that it certainly must be an extraordinary place! The splendor and glory of God's heavenly abode will be for us to enjoy as well. It is such a glorious place that Jesus referred to it as "paradise" (Luke 23:43). Paradise is a descriptive name for heaven connoting peace, tranquility, and perfection. Its grandeur cannot be fathomed this side of glory. Human intelligence does not have the capacity to comprehend its fullness. As Scripture points out, "What eye did not see and ear did not hear, and what never entered the human mind—God prepared this for those who love Him" (1 Corinthians 2:9).[17]

Heaven is nothing short of awesome. We will be awestruck throughout eternity with the contrast between heaven and our present earthly existence. As nice as this earth seems now, fallen creation does not begin to compare with the unadulterated grandeur that will surround us in heaven.

Secondly, Jesus said that He was preparing a place just for us (John 14:2). So, each of us already has a reservation at the grandest place in the universe—the eternal home of the righteous: "To everyone who is victorious I will give fruit from the tree of life in the paradise of God" (Revelation 2:7 NLT).

Thirdly, in heaven there will be inspiring worship. When we hear the question voiced by many, "What exactly are we going to be doing there?" we can affirm one thing for certain: Revelation chapter 19 says that we, along with the angels, are going to do a lot of praising God.

Notice the adjective "inspiring." If your worship preference is loud and exuberant, this is going to fit the bill. The Bible mentions that before the throne of God, the multitudes are going to be roaring in praise. The sound will be deafening, like mighty, crashing waves and rolling thunder. There will be no nodding off in this service! J.I. Packer says, "Hearts on earth may say in the course of a joyful experience, 'I don't want this ever to end.' But invariably it does. The hearts of those in heaven say, 'I want this to go on forever.' And it will. There will be no better experience than this."[18]

And there is a bonus. In Revelation 2:17 we read that everyone will be given a new name, known only to the Giver and the one who receives it. While our old names will still be valid, we believe God will have a special, intimate name for each of us, which He will use when communicating with us. Think of it as similar to the special communication that was enjoyed between God and Adam before sin marred that perfect relationship.

Fourthly, according to Revelation 20, we will also be appearing in front of God's judgment throne, where books will be opened and everything we ever did while here on earth will be examined. Galatians 6:7–9 says not to grow weary, for we will reap a harvest in eternity, which will reveal what we've planted in this life. We need to remember that we have only a short time in this life to do our planting. In Revelation we are told that we will be rewarded for our good works and that our sins will be declared "paid for" by Jesus' sacrifice, but only if our name appears in the Book of Life.

Fifth, we will enjoy good company. God will be there, Christ will be there, the angels will be there, the Church will be there, our believing family members and friends will be there, and the "spirits of just men made perfect" from all ages—according to Hebrews 12:23 (NKJV)—will be there. Who wouldn't want to enjoy that kind of company forever and ever? Our relationships will be deepened instead of broken.

There will be clear communication—perfect at all times and with everyone with whom we converse—instead of misunderstanding. Instead of stress and strained relationships with others, we'll experience emotional tranquility and harmony. Social needs will be fully met in perfect love, ecstatic joy, and eternal peace—the first three "fruit of the Spirit" (Galatians 5:22–23). Additionally, the other six fruit of the Spirit (patience, kindness, goodness, faith, gentleness, self-control) will naturally follow in perfect expression as well. This is how God intended mankind to live in society. What was lost in the Garden of Eden will be restored in heaven. All our relationships and social interactions will be pleasant and good!

Sixth, all pressing concerns, disappointments, and painful experiences in this life will be a thing of the past. They will simply be gone. John's glimpse of heaven details this:

> Then I heard a loud voice from the throne: Look! God's dwelling is with humanity, and He will live with them. They will be His people, and God Himself will be with them and be their God. He will wipe away every tear from their eyes. Death will no longer exist; grief, crying, and pain will exist no longer, because the previous things have passed away. (Revelation 21:3–4)

Seventh, we will finally see God face to face! The Almighty Creator of the universe will allow us to see Him in His splendor and glory. We will be awestruck as we look upon Him "in our righteousness." David says it this way: "But I will see Your face in righteousness; when I awake, I will be satisfied with Your presence" (Psalm 17:15).

Doing What in Heaven?

We know these changes will make for a glorious experience and existence. Now back to the question that is uppermost on our minds: What are we going to be *doing* the whole time we are there?

In his book *Heaven*, Randy Alcorn says that we must take what we know about God now and use our imagination to relate it to the future. Now, this can be an obstacle for many. Some of us have a difficult time dealing with present-day reality, let alone something we haven't seen. Alcorn tells about the difficulty Marco Polo had relaying to his contemporaries all the wonders he had seen and experienced in the court of Kublai Khan in China. The minds of thirteenth-century Italians were closed to the possibilities of his account, even though they lived during the same time period and in the same latitude and had similar resources. Like Polo's contemporaries, we have difficulty imagining anything could be better than what we now experience.[19]

A few years ago, I (Benny) traveled to an island in the South Pacific to visit my missionary brother (Marv). When I took my first snorkeling trip in the clear, tropical ocean, I could hardly believe the unseen, totally different world just a few feet below the surface. I was awestruck by the bright colors of the tropical fish and stands of brilliant coral. I sucked in a lot of water when my smile expanded past my mouthpiece as I discovered a completely different world for the first time. Here was a sterling underwater environment that had existed from the beginning of creation and yet was unknown to me until I had the opportunity to see underwater. Though I had seen fish in an aquarium, I never had the slightest conception of the beauty of the underwater world.

Likewise, even though we have a bit of information on heaven, we can't begin to imagine how good it really is going to be and how it will fill our time. But this doesn't mean we shouldn't try. In fact, we are instructed in Colossians 3:1–2 to set our hearts on things above, where Christ is.

We need to raise our sights and stretch our imaginations to comprehend how we will be filling our time there. Too often, we are limited in our perception of heaven by the caricatures that depict the heavenly experience as humans with angel wings, floating around on puffy white clouds and playing harps. Is it surprising that we wonder if we're going to be bored? One thing is certain: we are not going to have angel wings, do the work of angels, or even become angels, as is the misconception of some. God created the angels for a distinct purpose and human beings for another. They are two distinct orders. The two never become one and the same.

Remembers this: Satan wants us to avoid thinking about heaven, or—if we do try to imagine it—to distort its grandeur. Why? Because, as previously said, he's been there in the past, but, because of his rebellion, he got booted out. He knows how wonderful and awesome heaven really is, and is determined to create doubt and distortion in our minds. His goal is to cause a wedge between the Creator and us, especially in regard to the greatness of eternal glory.

Pleasures Forevermore

We also need to remember that God is the Creator of all good things, and that includes unadulterated pleasure. God created not only humans for His pleasure, but also the world for humans to enjoy. Presently, our sin prevents us from experiencing all the magnificent pleasure God has designed for us. However, in heaven that will not be the case. We will be the recipients of the full extent of the pleasures God originally designed for us. Pleasures will not be corrupted by sin as they are in our present experience. King David, reflecting on the glories of heaven, says in Psalm 16:11: "You make known to me the path of life; in your presence there is fullness of joy; at your right hand are pleasures forevermore" (ESV). Fullness of joy! Pleasures forevermore! This is another reason we'll be doing a lot of praising in heaven.

Think for a moment of one thing that brings you a great amount of joy. Now try to think of a way you could make it better. Realize that, while you were thinking, God could have come up with a thousand ways to enhance that joy beyond what you could ask or think, most of which would never have entered your mind.

Alcorn drives home the point that we'll enjoy these pleasures in the new heavenly body that each of us will possess. We will not be formless spirits, drifting aimlessly through God's heavenly realm. John, in Revelation chapter 21 saw physical gates and roads made of gold, all of which indicates that our spirits will be embodied. The good news is that, according to 1 Corinthians 15, these new bodies will be glorious, pain-free, sin-free, and incorruptible. Now that is something to look forward to!

At the point of death, we may feel a little tenuous about our imminent relocation to heaven, but it should actually be a time of unreserved anticipation. Our existence in the next life in heaven will be nothing short of glorious. We will be reborn into an existence of eternal conscience perfection. This is why heaven will be so glorious. Could there be anything better than that?

Near the end of his life, D.L. Moody wrote, "Soon you will read in the newspaper that I am dead. Don't believe it for a moment. I will be more alive than ever before!"[20]

Is this the perspective you have as you await your promotion to glory?

Study Questions

1. What concerns you the most about going to heaven?

2. What is one thing you would like to know about heaven before you arrive?

3. Besides God and family, who else would you like to meet in heaven?

4. What do you think heavenly worship is going to be like?

5. Do we have any responsibility to help others get to heaven?

6. Do you believe, as some do, that people become angels in heaven?

7. How sure are you that you are going to be there? On what do you base your answer?

What did Jesus say? Read John 3.
What else does the Bible say? Read Revelation 3; 19–22.

CHAPTER 8

The Broad Road Ends

Immediately after I lost sight of the old woman on the narrow road, I resumed my mysterious journey. Again I was pulled away from the road I didn't want to leave and deposited onto the thoroughfare I had begun to dread.

Again I had feeling that my hovering time was shortly coming to an end. As I landed on the superhighway, I could tell that something different was happening up ahead. The road was starting to decline at a sharper rate. I could see that the people were being funneled into a single lane marked "HELL DEAD AHEAD."

I looked into some of the faces and discerned that some people had a sense of apprehension, realizing that something out of the ordinary was in front of them. Their anxiety increased as they tried to slow their forward progress, only to have their efforts fail. Some grabbed tighter to all the things they had so cherished and spent their lives working for. But still the pace increased.

And then there it was, in crimson, smoking letters: a huge gate across the wide road, saying:

"YOU HAVE REACHED THE GATES OF HELL. YOUR
ROAD THROUGH ETERNITY CONTINUES HERE!"

The scenes at the end of the road varied. Some were violent: car crashes, falls, wars, criminal acts, and storms. Some were more expected: long illnesses and old age. All were unwelcome.

Just before they pitched headlong into the dreadful abyss, some people paused for a brief moment and looked back down the road they had traveled. Their faces registered despair as they realized they had spent their lives on the wrong road and now faced what was in store for them. Then they lost their grip on life and tumbled down and away.

Those who managed to grab the edge of the road and hang on for a few seconds with their fingertips were eventually pulled in by some ugly force. When I hesitatingly peered over the edge, I saw what it was: those same "pleasant guys" with the D ball caps. What had worn friendly faces on the road were now the most hideous things I could ever imagine. They were laughing and giving each other high-fives as they "helped" their victims one last time.

As I continued to peer over the edge, I saw a most terrible scene: people tumbling away from sight into a smoky haze—young and old, rich and poor, educated and ignorant, strong and weak, beautiful and ugly. It made no difference where they came from or who they had been. They were joined together in one common, screaming mass.

I could hear specific, piercing cries in the awful din:

"No, this can't be!"

"Help, save me!"

"But I'm a good person, I don't understand."

"Lord, Lord!"

"Mommy!"

"I went to church."

"Where did I go wrong?"

"God, I hate You!"

"But I believed I was on the right road, wasn't that enough?"

"This can't be right, I was baptized as an infant."

"It's so dark here, where is God?"

"It's worse than I could have ever imagined."

And the loudest and most prevalent screams were the most heart-sickening: "Why didn't someone tell me?"

My ears were assaulted with cursing, moaning, and squealing so awful that I had to put my hands over them. But this had little effect. All my senses were being assailed. The smell was so putrid I began to retch. My skin felt like every nerve was on fire. While I couldn't see through the darkness all the way into hell, what I *could* see was enough to know that nothing could be more horrifying.

I knew I had to get away from this holocaust or I, too, would be consumed by its evil. Thankfully, I felt myself being lifted up again into my hovering state. What a relief!

As I looked around, I could see that this end of the whole disk was full of people reaching the end of their broad boulevards, tumbling to their dreadful fate. I felt a sharp pain like a stab in the heart when I recognized a few of them as personal friends or acquaintances that I had met on the road. Further back, others were still traveling, completely oblivious to how close they were to this dreadful end. I felt a great compulsion to stand with my arms wide open to stop the impending disaster, but then I remembered that Someone had already done that and had been ignored by these travelers . . .

Reflection: Into the Abyss

On Christmas day in 1541, on the altar wall of the Sistine Chapel, Michelangelo revealed the largest fresco ever painted until that time, entitled *The Last Judgment*. He depicted Christ on His throne and mankind—separated into two groups, one going to heaven and the other going to hell—in front of Him. One small scene of this masterpiece is called "Despair," in which a distraught man realizes that his rejection of Christ has sentenced him to hell. His face is filled with anguish.

Mankind cannot begin to imagine how bad spending eternity in hell is going to be. Artists like Michelangelo have used their artistic talents to portray it, and writers have used thought-provoking words and imagination to help our minds grasp its horrors. In the 1300s Dante wrote his classic poem *Inferno* about the subject. Yet all of man's imagination pales in comparison to the reality of a place were the goodness of God does not exist and only evil reigns. As previously stated, the Bible gives us several descriptions of this ghastly place, and the story Jesus told of the rich man and Lazarus is frightening (see Luke 16:19–31).

There are several things we humans know by observation and some things we instinctively know. We know for sure that we are going to die. The only question is when. We instinctively know that there is something beyond the grave. The ancient Egyptians built the pyramids, Native Americans constructed mounds, and the Chinese had elaborate tombs stuffed with goods, all for the same purpose—to prepare for the afterlife. Throughout every era, the common man has been cremated or buried in a small grave. But no matter the culture or time in history, all hoped for an afterlife where they would experience enjoyment for all of eternity.

If the afterlife were just an old superstition, you would think that, by now, man would have moved beyond these beliefs and practices. But no, things have not changed since the beginning of time. All civilizations believe in an afterlife. *Why?* you might ask. There is only one answer that makes sense.

The One who created us with the ability to breathe without thinking also instilled in us the instinct to know there is eternal life. Just as He made a connection between our mind and our mouth, He put something in our heart that says to our mind, *Human existence doesn't end at death.* Solomon, the wisest and most enlightened man of all time, stated it plainly: "He has also set eternity in the human heart; yet no one can fathom what God has done from beginning to end" (Ecclesiastes 3:11 NIV).

Eternity has been set in our hearts. It is part of the very warp and woof of our being. God has put a spiritual homing device, like a GPS that directs our thoughts toward life after death, in each heart. We need to prepare for that which will assuredly come.

Study Questions

1. What are some common regrets people have expressed as they approached the end of their lives?

2. Does your earthly status is this life have any effect have any on what happens in the next? Why do you think Jesus so hard on the rich man?

3. Do you believe that eternity is stamped into everyone's heart? Have you met someone who denies this?

4. Reality check: Are you certain you are on the road to heaven?

   What did Jesus say? Read Matthew 25:31-46. Luke 16:19-21
   What does the Bible say? Mathew 3:11-12

Michelangelo's "Despair" part of the "Lastjudgment,"
on the front wall of the Sistine Chapel

CHAPTER 9

Voices in the Dark

I felt once again that now familiar but unsettling tug that always happened just before I was rushed off to another destination. I felt disappointment because, after the trauma that I had just experienced, I was hoping my traveling was finished. I instinctively knew that this particular jaunt was not going to be pleasant. In a nanosecond, I zoomed across the whole span of the flat disk below me, with its blurred masses of humanity, and then plunged steeply downward beyond its edge.

Immediately, it became so dark that I could feel the weight of the blackness crushing me. I found it difficult to breathe. I felt like I was on the bottom of the dreadful pile-on game that my dorm was known for in college. I tried to scream but didn't have the breath to do so. All I could manage was a pitiful wheeze. I felt I had fallen into a deep, black hole, where gravity was so dense that light couldn't penetrate it. The darkness was not only heavy but also evil—and dreadfully so. I repeatedly tried to brush it off myself, but to no avail.

Then, in an instant, I realized what had happened to me. I was dead! *How could this be!* I wanted to shout but couldn't because there was no air to do so. Already I missed that special gift of breathing and the pleasant rhythm of my body as it inhaled and then exhaled. How could something so ordinary in life suddenly become so precious after death?

Immediately a realization came to me: not only was my body dead, but my soul was in hell. Oh, the awfulness of this awareness! It didn't make any sense to me. Yes, I had just spent a lot of time on the broad

road that led to this destination, but I was just a spectator . . . or so I thought. *How did I end up in this dreadful place?* I questioned. I had no doubt that I was a follower of Jesus Christ and truly believed that His death on the cross for my sin and His victorious resurrection paid the penalty that should have kept me from coming to this awful place. I hoped with a fervent intensity that this was just a visit.

Not only was I being squashed by the darkness, but all my other senses were being assailed as well. The air was thick with a rancid smell that was so putrid I could taste it and began to gag. If pure evil had a scent and a taste, this had to be it.

I had become so distraught with my own situation that I had become deaf to the terrible din that surrounded me. But now that slowly became distinct. It was like standing in the center of a pitch-dark, outdoor athletic stadium filled with millions upon millions of people who were screaming as loudly as they could, but with one major difference: this was no cheer prompted by grand entertainment, no sound of encouragement, no pleading for something exciting and athletic to happen. Rather, all the voices were yelling in pain and agony at a decimal level that couldn't be measured!

I was so disoriented. The shouts of misery were coming from all directions: above, below, left, right, front, and back. In the deep darkness I couldn't tell if I was in my hovering state or standing on some unseen object. I was afraid to move in case I was on the edge of a precipice, poised to topple into a pit of greater wretchedness.

The volume of the deafening uproar seemed to be increasing. I tried pulling my hands up and pressing them against my ears to block out some of the noise, but to no avail. It seemed that each individual within the multitude encircling me had their own dedicated telephone line to the audio senses in my head. My skull felt like it was about to explode.

Just as I was about to lose hope of maintaining my sanity, my mind began to distinguish individual, tortured utterances. I began to concentrate on one voice at a time and found that, with some effort, I could "tune in" on one and faintly understand what was being said.

I heard an agonized voice bawl, "Why am I here? Why am I here? I was never a bad person. I lived my life pretty much by the golden rule. Please let me out. Why am I here?"

"Who are you?" I screamed through my thoughts. And then, for the first time, I realized that even though I was sure I was in hell, I was not experiencing any real physical discomfort. With the exception of the suffocating darkness and oppressive noise, I felt no distress, and had no reason to be screaming back at this voice. Maybe the worst was yet to come, but for now I felt a sense of relief.

"I am the unjustly sentenced," replied a feminine voice. "I led a good life, took care of my family, raised my kids well, volunteered for numerous groups, and never committed a serious crime."

"Did you worship God?" I inquired, this time without blaring.

"Does going to church on Christmas and Easter count? No, I guess not," the voice said in answer to her own question. "I never had much time for all that religious stuff. I thought I was good enough. There seemed to be so much religious diversity, it was all so confusing to me.

"Maybe if someone had explained it to me I wouldn't be here now," the voice sobbed. I couldn't help but feel sorry for her. I hoped she wasn't one of my friends in life, but I didn't recognize the voice.

"How long have you been here?" I spoke into the darkness, hoping that the voice was still "on the line."

"I have no idea. Maybe just a few minutes or maybe a hundred or even a thousand years. To me it seems like eternity," the voice replied. "Without a spark of light, there is no sense of time." The voice faded away in the darkness.

As that voice disappeared, the earsplitting screams of the multitudes returned. I made believe I was manipulating an old-fashioned radio dial, trying to tune in another individual voice out of the woeful mass. It took awhile, but I finally was able to single one out.

"Where's Bobby? Can you hear me, Bobby? If you're out there, Bobby, talk to me," the voice pleaded in agony.

"I'm not Bobby, but I would like to know about him," I said, cutting into the rant.

"Since you're not Bobby, I really don't want to talk to you. But I'll go ahead and do so since you are the only one who has ever talked back to me since I arrived here," the voice answered with contempt.

"So who's Bobby?" I asked, ignoring the disdain coming from the hateful voice.

"Bobby and I were best friends growing up. We had a lot of good times, but mostly enjoyed getting into trouble together. We often joked that someday we would go to hell together and continue our escapades with the devil himself." All of a sudden, the voice let out a piercing shout of intense pain. I instinctively recoiled from the intensity.

After allowing time for the voice to recover, I asked, "Are you sure that Bobby is here?"

"Oh, he's here all right," the darkly shrouded voice replied. "I saw him killed by a cop years before I arrived here. The darkness and the constant pain, the lack of anyone to talk to is excruciating. I'm almost enjoying talking to you." Then the voice began to break up. The last words I could discern were, "If you happen to meet up with Bobby, tell him to listen for me. I'm so lonely." And then the communication was lost.

As the shrieks of torment from the anonymous voices in the darkened sphere continued, I began to reflect on how different this hell was from the one I had always imagined—not that I had really spent a lot of time thinking about it. At any rate, it was different.

For instance, the little red demons jabbing their victims with pitchforks as they roasted in a roaring fire were nowhere to be seen. Nowhere did I see people being mutilated by wretched imps. Nor had I yet to encounter the devil with ivory horns and serpentine tail.

During my education I had been forced to read Dante's fourteenth-century *Divine Comedy: Inferno*. It must have had more influence in shaping my view of hell than I realized. So far, I hadn't seen any of the expected monsters; neither did I have a guide (like Virgil) to show me around; nor had I seen any of my enemies conveniently suffering various forms of torture. This darkness made all that impossible. All the jokes that I had told and listened to that made fun of those who ended up in this dreadful place now seemed horribly wrong. There was nothing funny about this situation.

In the dark, I thought I heard a giggle, but quickly dismissed it as my subconscious desire to hear some joy. Then I heard it again, and then again—and then a whole chorus of sinister voices joined in the revelry. I fine-tuned my listening skills and heard various exclamations: "Oh boy, here come some more. Don't they look surprised? I sure did a great job of deceiving that one. Won't the Prince be happy?"

As I reflected on this chatter, another single voice in pitiful agony pierced the chorus of pain.

"Lord, please, please give me another chance," it pled. If it were possible, this voice seemed to be suffering a little more than the others I had heard until now.

"Do you really believe that He will?" I asked into the dark.

"If He is the loving God that He is made out to be, He won't keep me here in agony for eternity," the voice whimpered.

"Do you think you deserve to be here?" I questioned the unseen voice.

"Of course I do, at least for a while. I'll admit that I used my political power to abuse and kill many people," the voice sobbed in pain. "But I did it only for a little while, and even though I don't know how long I've been here, I'm sure that it's been more than long enough to cover the wrongs I did when I was alive. And I do feel sorry for the ones I victimized."

"Don't listen to that awful creep," a different voice hissed out of the darkness. "That piece of scum had me killed and forced me to come here before my time. Maybe I would have changed my own course of life had I lived longer." Then he threatened, "If I can find you, I am going to make your pain even worse!"

This exchange shocked me, as this was the first time I had heard one voice address another. Granted, it wasn't a pleasant conversation, but it was something. I waited for more chatter between these two, but I could discern no more.

Once again I was assailed by the multitude of angry and tormented voices. Nothing I could do reduced the volume. At the very least, I expected to see the flames that caused such agony, but there was just rancid darkness. Maybe it wasn't flames at all that caused such torment. Maybe it was the absence of anything good. Maybe it was the absence of God. Maybe . . .

Suddenly, as I was pondering the possibilities, a tormented sound beyoud my imaginationrose out of the mass. Like the voice before it, this one was definitely in more agony than some of the others.

"Forgive me, Jesus, I know now that You are the Son of God, and only Your death and resurrection can keep people from coming to this God-forsaken place," the voice sobbed.

Am I hearing right? I wondered. This voice that, by the sound of its distress, was in more pain than the others was plainly acknowledging Jesus and asking for forgiveness. There was no way I could resist inquiring about this.

"Why are you being tortured in a way worse than others?" I asked.

"Because I always knew the truth," the new voice squealed in agony. "And not only did I fail to acknowledge Jesus for who He was as my Savior, but I kept others from knowing about Him, too."

"How did you do that?" I asked into the sea of darkness.

"Back when I was alive, I was an educated religious leader. But I critically rejected parts of God's Word, making it fit into what I thought was a less antiquated worldview. I foolishly tried to make God into something 'better.' I certainly didn't want to believe in a God of justice who permits people to come to a place like this." A long period of sobbing ensued, and then finally the voice continued.

"Now I realize that I was elevating myself and diminishing the holiness of God. Not only that, but I taught my erroneous beliefs to those who put their confidence in me as their religious father. Adoration became more important than truth. I am now suffering horribly for my misguided arrogance, and I fear that others who believed my teaching will experience the same fate."

"I heard you asking God for forgiveness. Do you think you will receive it?" I inquired.

"From what I know, probably not," answered the voice with great sorrow. "I had plenty of opportunities during my lifetime, and now I am paying a terrible price for not taking advantage of them. My only hope is that on the Day of Judgment, when we will all face Him, He will surprise us by doing something that was never mentioned or remotely indicated in His Word.

"My only other hope is that God will go back on what He has said and declare that suffering for eternity is too long—and that He graciously annihilates us on the spot. I think that's the best I can hope for. But deep down, I don't expect that to happen."

"I have one more question," I said. "I was expecting to see flames of fire torturing people, bringing them excruciating pain. I haven't seen any fire. What is causing the harm that everyone is screaming about?"

"I don't know what is causing my pain since it is impossible to see. But every time I think back on one of my sins," the voice continued, "I experience a pain that feels like a flaming sword stabbing me. And the hell of it all is that I can't stop thinking about my sins."

This single voice grew faint and the chaotic screaming bombarded me again. I was so exhausted from this whole experience that I felt as if every molecule in my being was becoming detached from all the others.

Just when I felt I couldn't take any more, a car's horn blared right next to me. It snapped me out of my stupor. What a relief! I found myself sitting at the round table, on the metal chair, instead of hovering above it. People were going in and out of the Starbucks without giving me a second look. How long I had be in my trance, I had no idea. As I watched them following by, I felt the urge to get up and ask them if they knew what road they were on. I quickly dismissed the thought, after all what business was it of mine?

Reflection: How Bad Is Hell?

Just the thought of hell is revolting to the human mind. Our senses are appalled at its very concept. We have a natural aversion to pondering what that dreadful place is like. Instead, we prefer to trivialize or minimize it. Many do so by telling light-hearted jokes about it or by using it as a common curse word. That's more palatable to us than facing the grim reality of a terror-invoking, permanent, final destination comprised of eternal suffering. Most of us would prefer to avoid the subject altogether.

But we can't.

The reason we can't is because of Jesus. For whatever reason, Jesus decided to tell us more about hell than heaven. He described its horrors in more detail than any other person in the Bible. So, if we feel uncomfortable with the subject, we must blame Jesus.

On second thought, instead of blaming Him, maybe we should express appreciation to Him for giving us a peek into a reality that lies beyond the grave; for telling us that the next life can be far worse than the present; for describing in graphic detail a place of horror beyond our wildest imagination. Yes, it seems more appropriate to thank Him than to fault Him for bringing credence to this subject.

The best way to delve further into this topic is by answering a series of questions that are commonly asked about it. The following questions are some of the most readily voiced and most relevant to this discussion.

1. Why did Jesus use such graphic symbolic language to describe hell?

    Even a casual reader of the works and words of Jesus as recorded in the four Gospels will note that Jesus was very graphic in describing hell. He used phrases such as "outer darkness," "lake of fire," "weeping and gnashing of teeth"; He described a place of torment where "the worm does not die," where "the fire is not quenched," and where one experiences eternal separation from the blessings of God. Jesus was not reticent at all in depicting the place that He knew a lot about in these terms, since He Himself created it.

But are these descriptions from Jesus to be understood as mere symbols, or are they to be taken literally? One of the best answers to this question comes from theologian R.C. Sproul. Here is what he says:

> I suspect they are symbols, but I find no relief in that. We must not think of them as being merely symbols. It is probable that the sinner in hell would prefer a literal lake of fire as his eternal abode to the reality of hell represented in the lake of fire image. If these images are indeed symbols, then we must conclude that the reality is worse than the symbol suggests. The function of symbols is to point beyond themselves to a higher or more intense state of actuality than the symbol itself can contain. That Jesus used the most awful symbols imaginable to describe hell is no comfort to those who see them simply as symbols.[21]

So, whether Jesus' graphic descriptions of hell were symbolic or not, He intended to convey to His listeners the wretchedness of that place—which leads directly to the next question.

2. Is hell really all that bad?

Those who prefer to trivialize hell's severity are usually the ones who raise this question. The thought behind the question is, "If I choose to ignore God and His standards and live a life outside of relationship with Him, will eternity without Him be all that bad? Frankly, I can live with that."

But, it must be remembered that Jesus referred to hell as not just bad, but terribly bad. He described it as a place of eternal, conscience punishment (Matthew 3:12; 18:8; 25:41, 46; Mark 9:43–48).

In Luke 16:19–31, Jesus tells a parable that graphically depicts the horrors of hell. We have already mentioned it back in chapter 1, but will again. It is about an unnamed, callous rich man who dies and goes to hell and a poor beggar named Lazarus who also dies but enters paradise. The rich man does not go to hell because he is rich, but because he shows no evidence of godly compassion or connection. In the parable, he lifts up his voice while in torment and first pleads for relief for himself; but when that is not granted, he pleads for the lives of his still living five brothers in the hope that they will not join him there. Why does he make such a plea? Because his experience in hell is bad—very bad—and he can not bear the thought of those he loved most experiencing its painful horror as well.

3. Does hell really continue forever and ever?

Every indication in Scripture makes clear that once a person dies and enters into hell, he will be there permanently (through all eternity). The Scriptures are in agreement on this topic (2 Thessalonians 1:9; Jude 7, 13; Revelation 14:11; 20:10, 15). Hell is not the obliteration or annihilation of a person that would shorten his existence there. Rather, it is the ongoing ruin in conscience existence outside of God's beauty and presence forever.

Some biblical scholars who have thought long and hard on this prospect have found the concept of eternal, conscience torment emotionally intolerable. They have therefore gravitated to the belief that an unbeliever's soul is extinguished at some future point, and thus will avoid punishment that goes on and on eternally. According to this line of thinking, the soul might be extinguished at the moment of physical death, or sometime in the future, after sufficient punishment for a sinful life is experienced. Punishment, according to this viewpoint, is extinction itself.

A well-known phrase that helps clarify that this cannot be the case is found at the end of John 3:16: "That whoever believes in him shall not perish but have eternal life" (NIV). At first glance, the phrase "shall not perish" might seem to support the idea that those who do not believe in Jesus will, in the end, be annihilated. After all, our common definition of the word "perishable" is something that is so fragile it is difficult to preserve. However, that is not the meaning behind this word. The word translated "perish" indicates divine condemnation, complete and ongoing, so that one is banished from its very opposite, eternal life.[22]

4. Is God present in hell?

    No, He is not.

    His judgment is there, but not God Himself. And this is the primary judgment that makes hell so abysmal—the complete and absolute absence of God. Dwell on that thought for a moment: existence outside of God's all-prevailing, providential, and caring presence. Separated from their Creator, unrepentant sinners will feel endless meaninglessness, worthlessness, and powerlessness. What a terrible judgment that is.

    Those condemned to hell will experience a dreadful God-void—emptiness as never, ever felt before. The Scriptures say it this way: "They will be punished with everlasting destruction and shut out from the presence of the Lord and from the glory of his might" (2 Thessalonians 1:9 NIV). The fundamental nature of hell is the absence of God. This aspect of judgment alone is hell enough.

5. Is not eternal punishment disproportionate to a finite life of sinning?

    This is a very good question, and one that has been asked by thinking people for quite some time. It is a good question because even our court system strives to protect offenders of the law from excessive punishment. In legal terms, an unwarranted penalty is referred to as "cruel and unusual punishment." In common language, the essence of this question is, "If I sin for only the duration of my lifetime (whether it be

30, 60, or 90 years), why would God go on punishing me forever and ever? Is that not excessive and unbalanced judgment?"

Surely, if we humans are astute enough to avoid over-punishing a wrongdoer, would not God be all the more? After all, one of the reasons He gave the Jews the civil laws found in the Old Testament was to guard against excessive punishment being administered to offenders. Now, if God was concerned enough to assure that safeguards be in place regarding temporal crimes, would He not do the same regarding eternal punishment?

One of the best answers to this question comes from the Puritan preacher Jonathan Edwards. Yes, this is a 250-year-old answer to what seems to be a contemporary concern, but Edwards faced the same objection in his day, and his answer is very insightful.

Edwards suggested that we should not consider how long one has sinned against God when measuring punishment, but rather how high and holy the person of God who is offended by one's sin. Since God is a being of infinite loveliness, infinite excellence, and infinite beauty, our sin and crime against Him is infinitely heinous and deserves infinite punishment.[23]

So, when considered from the vantage point of God's infinite personhood, infinite punishment is just. This is not disproportionate judgment. Based on God's holy character, it is judgment fully deserved. Second Thessalonians 1:5–6 states clearly that "God's judgment is right" and that "God is just" in administering it (NIV).

Another perspective on this question comes again from Sproul. Here is what he says:

No matter how we analyze the concept of hell it often sounds to us as a place of cruel and unusual punishment. If, however, we can take any comfort in the concept of hell, we can take it in the full assurance that there will be no cruelty there. It is impossible for God to be cruel. Cruelty involves inflicting a punishment that is more severe or harsh than the crime. Cruelty in this sense is unjust. God is incapable of inflicting an unjust punishment. The Judge of all the earth will surely do what is right. No innocent person will ever suffer at His hand.[24]

So again, based on God's goodness and His inability to be cruel, we know God judges rightly when He inflicts eternal punishment in the next life on those who have repeatedly offended Him in this life.

6. Are there degrees of punishment in hell?

In our story, the religious teacher experiences more pain and torment than the others. This raises the question: Are there "degrees" of suffering in hell? Do those who lived more wicked lives while on earth experience a harsher punishment than those whose lives were morally better? Are people judged in accordance with the amount of "light" available to them and their response to that light?

The idea that there are gradations in hell seems to be inferred from Scripture. Jesus implied as much in Luke 10:12–14 (NIV):

I tell you, it will be more bearable on that day for Sodom than for that town. Woe to you, Chorazin! Woe to you, Bethsaida! For if the miracles that were performed in you had been performed in Tyre and Sidon, they would have repented long ago, sitting in sackcloth and ashes. But it will be more bearable for Tyre and Sidon at the judgment than for you.

The "that day" Jesus refers to is the day of final judgment. That phrase, coupled with "more bearable . . . at the judgment," strongly indicates a distinction in judgment. Not all suffering in hell will be equal. Some sinners will be more severely punished than others. There will be appropriate discrimination.

7. Can the dead be converted?

Some may be thinking, "Okay, even if I am unwilling to believe in God and His gracious provision of salvation in this life, will I not have opportunity to do so after I die? Will there not be a second chance? Is there not opportunity for postmortem conversion?"

Nowhere in Scripture do we find the hope that a person is given a second opportunity once he has passed on from this life. Jesus' parable of the rich man found in Luke 16 and mentioned above confirms that there was no possibility for the condemned rich man to be relocated to the paradise side of eternity. Paul taught the same in several places; he affirmed that on Judgment Day, all receive a permanent destiny corresponding to the decisive direction of their lives (Romans 2:5–16; 2 Corinthians 5:10; Galatians 6:7–8).

A verse in Hebrews that affirms there will be no second opportunity after death for a person to repent is found in 9:27: "It is appointed for people to die once—and after this, judgment."

The writer uses the particular word "once" (*hapax* in Greek) that conveys "once and for all." It points to the decisiveness of the event. When it happens, it is a permanent happening, never to be repeated. Commenting on the finality of this term, J.I. Packer states, "The unrepeatable reality of physical death leads directly to reaping what we sowed in this world."[25] Death is final (contrary to reincarnation), and so is one's final destination following it.

Would a just-deceased person's perception of God and His grace differ from the perception he held when he was alive in the world and experiencing God's common grace? Would he change his mind about God and desire Him then? The narrative earlier in this chapter makes crying out to Jesus for deliverance seem a possibility. However, the Scriptures say nothing of God extending a second-chance grace and a second opportunity to the condemned deceased. And there is little indication of the condemned even wanting this. The lack of desire for God, for Christ, and for heaven in this life is indicative of a heart condition that is most likely unchanged in the next. That is why Packer suggests that "for God to extend the offer of salvation beyond the moment of death, even for thirty seconds, would be pointless. Nothing would come of it."[26]

Study Questions

1. What do you think the worst thing about being in hell would be?

2. The reality of hell permeates the teaching of Jesus. Can you pinpoint some of those teachings?

3. If the biblical descriptions of hell are symbolic, then would the reality be worse than the symbols?

4. Is there no cruelty in hell? How can it be a place of perfect justice?

5. Is there escape from hell either through repentance or annihilation?

6. Do you believe there are different punishments in hell?

What did Jesus say? Read Matthew 8:11–12; Mark 9:42–48; Luke 16:19–31.
What else does the Bible say? Read Jude 3–13; Revelation 20:11–15.

CHAPTER 10

Changing Your Final Destination

Since life goes on and on and on forever and ever, what is it going to be like for you after you physically depart this life and enter eternity? This story has been an attempt to graphically portray, as accurately as possible, the distinction between only two possibilities—that is, two paths that are so starkly different that God's great desire is that you choose just one—the one that leads to heaven with Him. He is not willing that any—including you—should perish and spend eternity apart from Him in everlasting judgment.

The only way to heaven is by accepting Jesus as your Savior. He alone can save you from the hell that is rightfully deserved by every sinner. You must make the choice of either believing in and accepting God's provision for your sin or not believing and rejecting it. Our hope for you, and the reason for this book, is that you come to realize your need to choose Jesus Christ today before your life's journey ends.

YOU CAN CHANGE YOUR FINAL DESTINATION. Here is how:[27]

1. First, admit you are a sinner.

We are all born into sin. We all have sin at the very core of our being. We are born under the power of sin's control. We can't help but commit sinful acts; sin is part of our very fabric as human beings. You inherited this sinful state from Adam, the first human being and the first to sin. The Bible says it this way: "For all have sinned and fall short of the glory of God" (Romans 3:23 NIV).

Your sin separates you from God, who is holy. And since He is perfectly holy, He cannot permit the filth of sin in His presence. You are therefore doomed to an eternity separated from Him. In order to be saved from the wrath to come, you must first admit that you are a sinner.

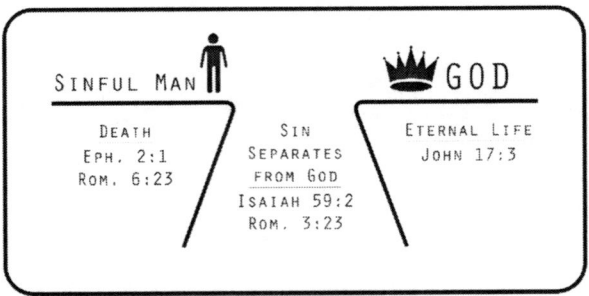

The price you pay for sin is heavy indeed. Not only do you face physical death, but also spiritual death, an even worse consequence. That death alienates you from God and will last through all eternity. The Bible teaches that this place that is separated from God is called hell. This is where unrepentant people will spend eternity. The Bible says it this way: "For the wages of sin is death, but the gift of God is eternal life in Jesus Christ our Lord" (Romans 6:23 NIV).

2. Second, recognize that you can do nothing to earn God's favor.

Man naturally tries to bridge the gap between his sinfulness and God's holiness by his own efforts. This is a universal phenomenon, and every religion, aside from Christianity, teaches its adherents to exert themselves by doing good works and deeds in order to be accepted by God. Yet, salvation is by grace, based on God's work on your behalf, because none of your efforts, no matter how intense, how sincere, or how regular can ever bridge the great divide between yourself and our holy God. You must recognize that you can do nothing to earn God's favor: "For it is by grace you have been saved, through faith—and this not of yourselves, it is the gift of God—not by works, so that no one can boast" (Ephesians 2:8–9).

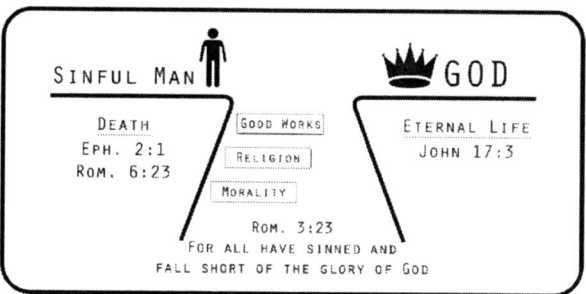

3. Third, accept Jesus as your Savior.

Because Jesus was not only fully man, He was also fully God and lived a perfect, sinless life. When He died on the cross, He bore mankind's sin, including yours, on Himself. He took the wrath of God for your sins upon Himself as your substitute. This means that He died in your place. And although He died many years ago, because He is the eternal God, His death is applied to all generations—including the present one. He died for you. This truth is summarized in John 3:16, 18 (NIV):

> For God so loved the world that he gave his one and only Son, that whoever believes in him shall not perish but have eternal life.

> Whoever believes in him is not condemned, but whoever does not believe stands condemned already because they have not believed in the name of God's one and only Son.

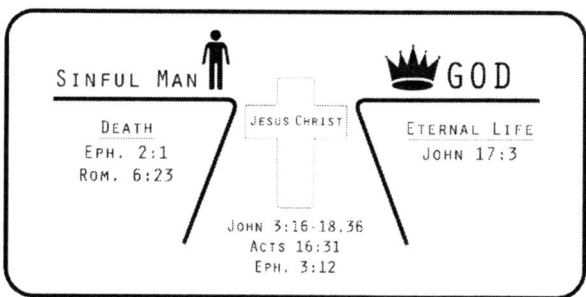

111

4. Fourth, rest in the assurance that you have eternal life.

You need do nothing more than, by faith, believe in Jesus as your own Savior. Once you have done that, you will experience an amazing transformation. Your outlook on life will change. Jesus will be Lord of your life—of your thoughts, desires, worldview, and conduct—and increase as such as you mature in your walk with Him. You will love Him and His ways more and more.

But just as importantly, you now have unwavering assurance that you will enter His presence in glory when your life on this earth has come to an end: "And this is the testimony: God has given us eternal life, and this life is in his Son. Whoever has the Son has life; whoever does not have the Son of God does not have life" (1 John 5:11–12).

No wonder this is called "Good News"!
Welcome to the family of God.
Welcome to eternal life.
Welcome to a changed and glorious final destination!

One Last Word...

Life with Christ is most gratifying and sustained when it is lived out in conjunction with other believers. If you try to stand alone in your newfound faith, you will probably fail. So, find a good church where other believers can encourage you. It is important that you find one that firmly believes in the Word of God—a place where it is preached, taught, and honored. It might take some time and effort on your part to find such a church, but the benefits will be well worth it.

There are many good Bible and Christian living helps online as well. Discover these for yourself and use them. Contact us if you need some direction. It would be our honor to be of help and to know you have made this most important decision. We will be willing to pray for you as well. Contact us through our website.

Looking forward to seeing you in heaven.

Notes

1   May 10–13, Gallup Poll on Religion.

2   *Truth Magazine*, July 17, 2003.

3   C. S. Lewis, *The Screwtape Letters* (New York: MacMillan, 1962).

4   John Wesley, The Journal of Rev. John Wesley Volume VI.

5   John Blanchard, *Whatever Happened to Hell?* (Evangelical Press: Durham, 1993).

6   C.H. Spurgeon andTom Carter, "Spurgeon At His Best" Grand Rapids MI: Baker,1991,67.

7   http://www.christianpost.com/news/apologist-debunks-all-religions-are-fundamentally-the-same-claim-33268/#yYhEXTh51EXTkrcf.99

8   Ravi Zacharias, *Jesus Among Other Gods*, NashvilleTn:Word Publishing,7.

9   Marvin Newell, *Commissioned: What Jesus Wants You to Know as You Go*, 130–131.

10 Dean C. Halverson, *The Compact Guide to World Religions*, Ada MI: Bethany House 1996, 29.

11 C. S. Lewis, *Mere Christianity* (MacMillan: New York, 1967).

12 C. S. Lewis, *The Problem of Pain* (Macmillan: New York, 1962), 118.

13 *Time Magazine*, April 14, 2011.

14 Albert Mohler, www.albertmohler.com/2011/03/16/we-have-seen-all-this-before-rob-bell-and-the-reemergence-of-liberal-theology/.

15 W.P. Strickland, *Autobiography of Peter Cartwright, the Backwoods Preacher* (New York: Carlton and Porter, 1857), 192.

16 Ligon Duncan, "Speaking Seriously and Sensitively about Hell to the Sons of this Age and the Next," March 15, 2011, reformation21.org.

17 Although the context of this verse deals with God's wisdom, it certainly applies to His works as well.

18 Randy Alcorn, *Heaven* (Tyndale: Carol Stream, 2004), 198.

19 Ibid., 15

[20] Bonnie H. Harvey, *D. L. Moody: The American Evangelist* (Barbour Books: Uhrichsville, 1997).

[21] R.C. Sproul, "Hell," http://www.bible-researcher.com/hell6/html.

[22] The Greek word is *apollumi*, which carries the twin ideas "to be lost" and "eternal destruction," as noted from the context of verse 17. (*Theological Dictionary of the New Testament*, edited by Gerhard Kittel, vol. 1, pp. 394–396.)

[23] Jonathan Edwards, "The Justice of God in the Damnation of Sinners," in *The Works of Jonathan Edwards*," vol. 1 (Edinburgh: Banner of Truth Trust, 1974), 669.

[24] http://www.bible-researcher.com/hell6/html.

[25] J.I. Packer, "Can the Dead Be Converted?" *Christianity Today*, January 11, 1999: 82.

[26] Ibid.

CPSIA information can be obtained at www.ICGtesting.com
Printed in the USA
LVOW07s2353290915

456014LV00002B/5/P